NANO HOUSE

NANO HOUSE

PHYLLIS RICHARDSON

INNOVATIONS FOR SMALL DWELLINGS

WITH 358 ILLUSTRATIONS, 335 IN COLOUR

 Thames & Hudson

To Hannah Flinders, with large-scale gratitude

Phyllis Richardson is the author of numerous books on
interiors, design and architecture, including the XS series,
three titles in the StyleCity series (Barcelona, London and Paris),
Contemporary Natural, House Plus and Living Modern,
all published by Thames & Hudson. She lives in London.

On the cover: (front) One+ Minihouse, Add-A-Room
(Matti Marttinen); (back, top to bottom) Blob, dmvA Architecten
(Frederik Vercruysse); Roll-It, Institut für Entwerfen und Bautechnik,
University of Karlsruhe (Sebastian Salopiata); Villa Hermina,
HŠH Architekti (Ester Havlová); Sunset Cabin, Taylor Smyth
Architects (Ben Rahn/A-Frame Inc).
On pages 2–3: Villa Hermina, HŠH Architekti (Ester Havlová)

First published in the United Kingdom in 2011
by Thames & Hudson Ltd, 181A High Holborn,
London WC1V 7QX

Copyright © 2011 Thames & Hudson Ltd, London

Designed by Peter Dawson, www.gradedesign.com

British Library Cataloguing-in-Publication Data
A catalogue record for this book is available from
the British Library

ISBN 978-0-500-34273-2

Printed and bound in China by Toppan Leefung Printing Ltd

To find out about all our publications,
please visit **www.thamesandhudson.com**.
There you can subscribe to our e-newsletter,
browse or download our current catalogue,
and buy any titles that are in print.

CONTENTS

INTRODUCTION

SPACE-SAVING IDEAS

Now that energy-efficiency is something most people are learning to get their minds around, the idea that we might be able to live with both less consumption and less built space is striking some as a reasonable corollary to the conversation about using and creating energy wisely. If we can send a man to the moon, an argument might go, we should be able to heat our houses without endangering the planet. But thinking about that trip to the moon could inspire other ideas, such as the concept of the amount of enclosed space a person actually needs to cater to the everyday functions, and some luxuries, of life.

Nobody is suggesting that we should all take up collapsible and fully recyclable housing, or indeed try to live in something similar in size to a space craft. While there are certainly examples of earthbound populations who live with minimal structural shelter — the yurt, for example, has been happily used for millennia — most of us in the developed world have become accustomed to a less rugged daily existence. Further, it is not often a successful tack to suggest that humans eschew advances in technology (and comfort) to address a future impact that may be hard to imagine. Make the efficient use of space also more attractive, more useful, more satisfying, and you are more likely to appeal to the better instincts even of those who still prefer cathedral ceilings or whose definition of luxury is turning on the central heating on cool summer mornings.

The aim of this book is not just to showcase a collection of well-designed small houses, tiny houses, or what we happily call 'nano houses'. We want to draw attention to structures that demonstrate a resounding appreciation for space, resources and materials through their effective use on a small scale. Some of the houses might be described as quirky or experimental, while others offer a more traditional approach. But all should provoke a discussion about design, efficiency, sustainability, proportion, harmony, function and necessity. Here is a survey of more than forty projects from around the world that rethink the feasibility of minimal living space in terms of all of those elements, and ask if perhaps we can do things better, even as we do them smaller.

For these reasons we have not chosen the standard building types, such as a tiny log cabin or a boat interior. These are both typologies that make good use of minimal space, and that cater to the needs of daily life with a sense of economy that is well worth examining in any discussion of more efficient housing. And some examples of each type do appear in these pages. But in the spirit of innovation and experimentation, in asking worthwhile questions about where we are and what we hope to achieve in terms of better building, the houses in this selection all have something new to suggest, or at least to contribute to the debate, on improving both the quality of housing and the use we make of our resources.

Perhaps no-one has written more precisely, or more famously, on the minimal requirements of habitation than Le Corbusier. In his view, the function of a house was to provide: '1. A shelter against heat, cold, rain, thieves and the inquisitive. 2. A receptacle for light and sun. 3. A certain number of cells appropriated to cooking, work, personal life.' It's a stark recipe, indeed, but of course all recipes have room for new ingredients. Le Corbusier also claimed that all we really need 'is a monk's cell, well lit and heated, with a corner from which [we] can look at the stars'. Here he may have been talking about his own meticulously designed, and surprisingly romantic, little 'cabanon' that he had built on the French Riviera as a retreat for himself and his wife. The furnishings are all tidily built in and can be folded away. It is a cosy, even homey, little habitation, handily sited next to the master's favourite restaurant, which could provide meals in case the diminutive kitchen proved too fussy to work in.

It is easy to laugh at Le Corbusier's extreme vision, but as with any popular or much-copied concept, it is often a good idea to go back to the original, to forget the poor imitations, and find the kernel of truth that appealed to people in the first place. Most of us in the developed world could live with less than we have and still have a greater degree of comfort, pleasure, even luxury, than is strictly necessary. In this way of thinking, stripping down to essentials is a starting point, not an end in itself, and it

is in the building back up again that we can find some exciting alternatives to our current demands. When you start from scratch, you can end up with amazing variety. Who needs to begin with four walls, or even a rectilinear form? If you're trying to maximize interior space, your external form might have to be a bit more adventurous. At least it's worth exploring the options.

The five chapters here each focus on different typologies of housing that could apply to much larger models. But in these pages all of the buildings have an internal area of under 75m² (807 sq ft), with many under 50m² (538 sq ft). The first chapter shows actual built houses that are used for family living. Chapter 2 contains structures that can be moved, whether they stand on wheels, float on water, are liftable by crane or, in one example, can be rolled on its side to a new site. Chapter 3 shows 'micro-retreats' that are perhaps the easiest to accept as small spaces, as they were all built for weekend or holiday use. Chapter 4 focuses on dwellings that take energy efficiency as their primary goal, and Chapter 5 is about housing that can be applied in multiples, whether for leisure or addressing the more serious challenges of affordable housing for the poor or emergency shelter for the dispossessed.

As ever in such a collection of projects, there will be some overlap, with houses appearing in one chapter that could easily fit in other categories. The purpose, however, is not to limit the scope of any of these designs, because even when talking about living with less, the idea is to open up the debate and expand our knowledge of, and interest in, what might be possible in the future and what has already been made possible by the creative minds at work here and now.

1

BUILT
COMPACT
HOUSES

Many people, when asked to imagine living in a house that has an interior of under 75m² (807 sq ft), can conceive of 'getting by', but few would imagine that the house might be in any way luxurious, or even an object of high design. The projects in this chapter disprove the notion that living small is living with less. There may be less open space, but the clever use of what space is available and the careful arrangement of functions almost defy their diminutive aspect.

These houses all demonstrate that using less space doesn't mean cramming amenities into uncomfortable quarters, and that innovation can be much more expansive, within limited measurements, than many would expect. They experiment with levels, like the Villa Hermina (p. 014) in the Czech Republic, which seems to present all of the interior on a slant, but in reality provides a very rational space at each level with ramps that offer more flexibility of use than solid, space-grabbing staircases. The House in Hiro (p. 018), in Japan, uses all of the available volume of its site to make way for outdoor spaces that bring in light, and for indoor spaces that help create the feeling of a garden.

There are houses that show a new attention to materials and planes, as in BAK Arquitectos' Casa XS (p. 022) in Argentina, which deviates from the local woodland dwellings with its bold material gestures and imaginative openings for natural light. House Lina (p. 036) in Austria extends the floor plane, which curves up to form an enclosed deck, and bends the roof plane so that it becomes part of the external wall. In some cases the solution is a compact, prefabricated, modular unit, such as the L41 (p. 032) in Canada, which is designed to be constructed in a factory, with the plan capable of being expanded and designed with the potential to create 'stackable' multi-unit complexes. The One+ Minihouse (p. 052) works on the traditional model of the Swedish summer retreat, which is often composed of several small buildings. The One+ Minihouse is an improvement on that idea, with structures that can be used as stand-alone houses, or connected to form larger dwellings.

Then there are remakes of older forms, a re-'wrapped' trailer home in Colorado is worlds away from the 'Forest for a Moon Dazzler' in Costa Rica, but both represent rethinking the familiar. The TrailerWrap house (p. 042), a project by students at the University of Colorado–Boulder, was a new approach to the old, unloved mobile trailer home, a way to maintain its basic efficiency while improving on the quality of materials and interior space. The Moon Dazzler house (p. 048) uses local materials and traditional methods, but in a new, modern form that is still effective in its environment.

Though some of these houses are intended for recreational use, they are all equipped for full-time, year-round habitation, with the range of services needed, and also offer a host of amenities that aren't always included in much greater square footage, such as clean, modern, light-filled interiors, outdoor decks, advanced appliances, energy-efficient construction and, in at least one case, a full view of the moon. Such a variety of perks certainly argues against the idea that inhabiting less space impedes a high quality of living.

A FILMIC SLANT

VILLA HERMINA
HŠH Architekti
Cernín, Czech Republic
59m² (635 sq ft)

This house, say the architects, 'has had a long genesis'. The concept sprang from a project developed for an exhibition entitled Space House, held in Prague in 1999, which drew the attention of a client who wished to build a family home that would also be 'an original work of art'. Over the next ten years, client and architects discussed a range of solutions, finally settling on this highly unusual angular design, with an interior that is both flexible and finely tuned. The lengthy discussions came about partly because the original exhibition contained six different designs, variations on spatial concepts that emphasized the designers' belief that the physical space is often neglected in contemporary buildings, due to a focus on other elements such as light or materials. Granted, the consideration of space seems a bit obvious to merit ten years of discussion, but a careful look at the result of those talks illustrates something of what the trio at HŠH were getting at.

The first two things that grab one's attention when looking at this project are the slant and the render, a sort of pink marshmallow material that makes the house look even less serious than the cocky angle implies. The exterior, however, is simply explained by the twin forces of practicality and inspiration. The render is a polyurethane spray that has effective thermal and damp-resistant qualities, while the colour is a reference to the designers' favourite building, Ludwig Leo's Versuchsanstalt für Wasserbau und Schiffbau in Berlin, with its giant external pipework painted in pastel pink. But it's the internal spaces of this house that are really intriguing. Inside, two standard levels are diagonally traversed by ramps that add more floor space,

but also provide access to the main levels and to storage (rather than a stairway, which is only an access route). Here another striking hue – bright green – becomes something of a mask of false whimsy: the spaces are logical and adaptable, with ingenious compartments and fittings that change according to the needs of the user. Such a degree of flexibility requires thought and planning for each step through the house, from the children's room and study on the lowest level to the cantilevered master bedroom at the top of the house. Kitchens and bathrooms are sited on comfortingly horizontal planes, while seats are suspended from the ceiling and a projector pops out of the lower ramp, creating a perfectly angled venue for cinema viewing.

This last feature was no accident, as the incorporation of the natural slope into the house was not merely a show of virtuosity. The client is a self-proclaimed lover of film, and a key part of the brief was to provide a room for screening movies with professional-level equipment. In this way, the architects put the slant of the site to very good use. But the grade actually reaches 21 per cent, so however useful the slope in creating a nicely raked seating area for at-home movie viewing, even they concede that it is 'quite an experimental dimension for housing'. Set at the edge of a village and on a steep hillside, the house also offers some extraordinary views to the outside landscape. The design is judicious in its use of windows (each wall has only one), but a large opening at the bottom of the second ramp offers both the look and feel of sliding off the mountain, an altogether heady effect for a house that questions the very shape and dimensions of domestic space.

Floors are covered in an anti-skid material usually found in sports facilities — no doubt necessary, given the house's sharp inclines. Kitchen and dining spaces are on a level horizontal plane.

'The internal arrangement does not allow for the placement of standard furniture, but amplifies the intensive spatial experience, the perception of every movement and the proximity of family members.'

The master bedroom –
actually only a bed – has been
cantilevered on the highest
level in the open space over
the ramp, like a ski jump.
Its frame becomes handy
bookshelves. Elsewhere, niches
are used for bunkbeds and
more storage.

SECRET GARDEN

<u>HOUSE IN HIRO</u>
Suppose Design Office
Hiroshima, Japan
66.5m² (710 sq ft)

It is difficult to imagine how steel, concrete and glass could be made to exude warmth and intimacy, but this small house is a lesson in how hard materials can be softened with economy of scale and generosity of natural light. Suppose Design Office are a prolific practice with many beautifully formed houses in their repertoire, along with shops, offices and interiors. Their designs have a certain tactile delicacy, as seen in the lengths of wood that reach up to form branches of a leafless tree for a bar in Hiroshima, or a house that looks as if its roof had been made from nothing more than crisply folded paper. In their designs for larger dwellings, there is nothing that is sprawling or monolithic, even when the main element might be unfinished concrete.

In this house in Hiro, the architects knew that they had to create a sense of comfort and beauty where there was none. Located in a shopping district alongside the main highway, the site is, as they put it, 'a harsh place to satisfy the demands of a client who desires a home with bright gardens'. Having designed houses that are partly underground, or whose rooms are reached by catwalks or varying levels of parallel planes, the team immediately fell to work on the entire vertical volume of the available space. Rather than thinking floor by floor, they looked at shafts of light and shadow, at how far and well light could be made to penetrate, by keeping things simple and open and by reducing both the materials and the obstacles that would be clad in them to a minimum.

As there was no room for an outdoor garden, the architects decided to 'plan the kind of place that one could almost call a real garden, by bringing indoors the materials that evoke elements of the outdoors'. This was accomplished

The use of untreated concrete and stone tiles helps to convey the theme of an indoor garden, while natural wood warms up the living space. Daylight from the atrium reaches the upper rooms through unglazed internal openings. Courtyard spaces at each end, though small, have a large impact on the light and atmosphere of the interior spaces.

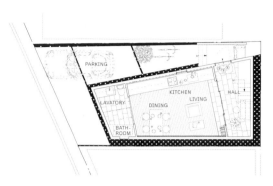

by making spaces for plants and bicycles alongside the living areas where furnishings, books, artwork and pianos are usually found. In doing this, they say, 'we have portrayed a life in which these elements, indoors and outdoors, are mingled'. This is all well and good, until one finds a draughty open-plan that lacks cohesion. But in this house, the cohesion comes with the small size and the limited palette of materials, as well as the brilliant linking of the two floors via the light-filled courtyard area at one side and the atrium-like bathing space at the other, which receives light from an open terrace off the bedroom above.

The kitchen core of the house is lined by fine strips of wood on both the floor and ceiling. The judicious choice of materials keeps this central core, with its paucity of natural light, wrapped in the comforting embrace of wood, while the areas at either end, which receive direct sunlight, can afford to be dressed in hardy slate and formworked concrete. There the stairs, always a potential obstacle to sightlines and natural light, emerge as wafers of Corten steel, protruding from the concrete outer wall. Such a floating effect with these industrial materials is a tribute to the architects' skill at making forms that belie their solidity and structural necessity. Though the demand for 'bright garden spaces' might seem challenging for a plot of this size and location, for the architects it revealed itself to be a prized opportunity to make lightness and warmth out of darkness and density.

IN WOODS AND WATER

CASA XS
BAK Arquitectos
Mar Azul, Argentina
52m² (560 sq ft)

The resort of Mar Azul lies about 400km (249 miles) north
of Buenos Aires, and offers a temperate blend of mild
weather, thick forest and pristine beach. It is a popular
area, but is still protected from overdevelopment. The site
for this small holiday cottage was a narrow strip of land,
set in the woods, but right up next to a 5m (16 ft) drop in
the sandbank. This provided obvious constraints, but also
some enviable opportunities for a private vista overlooking
the pine forest below. The architects took the clients'
sensitivity to the natural surroundings seriously, as well
as the request for a house of only 50m² (538 sq ft) or so.
There were other restrictions too: the house needed to
have as little impact on the site as possible; it had to be
viable within a small budget; and the construction time
needed to be brief, due to the remoteness of the site. Lastly,
the clients wanted something that would be easy to maintain
for years to come.

Even within these limits, the BAK team managed to
come up with something experimental, modern and yet
remarkably well suited both to the landscape and to the
demands of the clients. For all Modernist aficionados, the
house has a comfortable resemblance to a Miesian glass
pavilion. There is also a heavy reliance on the virtue of a
few, well-used materials. The primary materials are all
out in the open — concrete, wood, glass and some anodized
aluminium — but they each seem to inhabit a different formal
dimension. The concrete walls and roof keep to rectilinear
planes, except where the roof over the bedroom turns up
and over in a sort of inverted L-shape to accommodate the
slim, glazed section that separates the bathing/sleeping

The intentionally overlarge door opening was meant to mark the division of the interior spaces and overcome a sense of the diminutive, while at the same time adding a feeling of luxury to the minimal structure. Narrow vertical windows echo the rhythm of the trees in the forest beyond.

'Beyond the clear Modernist formula, there are twists and innovations that make this little house a pleasing puzzle of openings and sightlines.'

area and the living/dining space. This formal change was an important part of the design, not only to divide private from public areas in such a small structure, but also to break up the flow of materials and natural light. As the house sits in a group of other vacation cottages, the need for privacy inspired the blank façades at three sides, with the narrow sections of window and clerestories keeping the interior from feeling like a dark box.

The concrete helped meet several requirements at once. It was quick and easy to use, and was formed from a specially composed aggregate that included plastic, so that damp would not be a problem. The composition of the concrete also needed only a minimal amount of water for mixing, useful in an area where the fresh water supply is limited. Lastly, the material could be varied slightly for different effects. The floors are highly polished, while the walls, roof and supports have a boardmarked surface that mimics the planks of hardwood used elsewhere in the house and on the exterior decking. Despite its versatility, the architects were all too aware of concrete's more industrial associations, and were careful to insert glass (and natural light) in as many creative ways as possible, while still maintaining private internal spaces. The use of hardwood also helped to add layers of warmth and avoid 'a monotone atmosphere', inappropriate for a family home. But the layers of planes and internal partitions already alleviated any boxiness in the design. Like the surrounding forest, the house changes with the moving light.

NEW TRADITIONALIST

XXS HOUSE
Dekleva Gregorič Arhitekti
Ljubljana, Slovenia
43m² (463 sq ft)

For architects whose first commissions come from their own parents, the pressure to succeed must be intensified, but when those parents are architects themselves, the intensity must be of a different order. In the mid-1990s, Alijosa Dekleva's mother and father moved to the countryside but bought a rundown building in Krakovo, a small medieval area of Ljubljana. The property, built originally as the barn for a nearby house, was viewed partly as an investment and partly as a place for the parents to settle when they became less capable of driving and would need amenities closer to hand. In the meantime, the couple wanted a place to use when they visited the capital on weekends.

Though Dekleva's father continued to design and build houses, including a new country residence for himself and his wife, he left the redesign of the little barn to Dekleva and his partner, Tina Gregorič. Within the grander sprawl of Ljubljana, Krakovo is a pocket of traditional Slovenian village life. Until the end of the 19th century, its purpose was to provide food for the nearby monastery. Today, it retains its villagey atmosphere: houses are low rise, with the double-pitched roof typical of the area's rural dwellings, and many houses still keep small gardens. The challenge for the young architect was to design something in keeping with the scale, indeed the very size, of the previous building, as well as the basic vernacular, while creating a modern, light-filled retreat for his parents to enjoy on weekends and eventually as a full-time residence.

Bringing more light into the house was one of the most important requests of the brief that Dekleva received. The previous house had only two windows, so adding more would be one obvious solution; another would be to add a small atrium off the living space. Since local heritage regulations allowed for dormer windows, Dekleva and Gregorič exploited the possibilities of bringing in natural light from above, and made an open staircase so that light could also permeate the ground floor. Having successfully illuminated the interior, and then provided for the required spaces, the architects were given a free hand with materials by the client, though the local authorities required some convincing. The duo decided to retain the modest character of the former outbuilding (though adding more window openings), while innovating with materials where they could. The external cladding of fibre-cement panels, for example, are, Gregorič explains, a 'tribute' to the corrugated roof tiles that are common in the region. As used here, she continues, 'they are straight instead of corrugated, and the roof material comes down and also forms the cladding'. This use of a single material was intended to help retain the 'service' appearance of the building.

But while Dekleva's architect father had made his own requirements known from the beginning, his mother weighed in with a request for the interior. When considering what material to use for the floor surface, Dekleva says, 'we proposed resin, but finally agreed with my mum's idea for a terrazzo floor'. They then decided to go one better, deciding to use the terrazzo on the kitchen counters and sink as well. Getting the balance right between historic reverence and modern innovation is never easy. Striving also to take on parental demands alongside personal creative aims seems an even nobler ambition. This is a little house project that quickly filled with great expectations, and it seems they were well met.

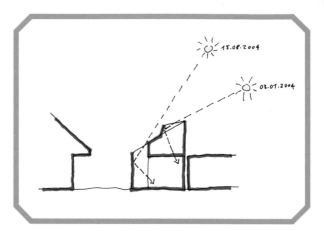

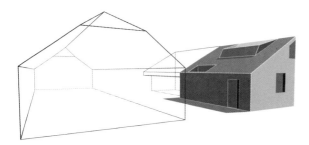

The architects favoured 'raw' materials: unpainted fibre-cement panels for the exterior; béton brut, plywood, iron and felt for the interior.

The scheme includes a careful arrangement of upper-floor windows, large glass doors and a small atrium to bring in as much sunlight to the little house as possible. The white-painted interior also enhances the effect of natural light.

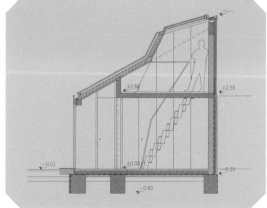

A MODEST PROPOSAL

L41
Michael Katz, Janet Corne
Vancouver, British Columbia, Canada
23m² (248 sq ft)

It started with a well-designed kitchen. 'In most subcompact units,' says architect Michael Katz, 'the kitchen is the first thing to be compromised. But we started with a fully equipped, highly functional kitchen...and from there, the rest easily followed.' But Katz's minimal, high-design, modular home has a lot more to its credit than a satisfying culinary capacity within a compact structure. As a model of living small, the L41 was meant to address far bigger concerns. Katz says that he felt that the question to ask was not just 'How small can a unit be?', but 'How small can a unit be before it ceases to be delightful?' He also seemed to be asking how it could help save the planet, provide shelter for its poorest inhabitants, and help promote a more equitable society.

The L41 is a stackable housing solution that draws inspiration from architect Moshe Safdie's Habitat 67 at Expo 67 in Montreal, an arrangement of 354 cubes that formed 148 residences. The basic L41 is a single, studio-style habitat intended for one person or a couple, but it can be expanded to accommodate a small family. Katz also hopes that it will be produced in quantities to form higher-density housing in flexible apartment buildings along the lines of Habitat 67, but with a far greater degree of sustainability in its materials and services. It addresses the issues of global warming and pollution, and those closer to home by making use of local wood that was in need of harvesting, due to damage from pine-beetle infestation. Katz has spent forty years designing objects (including the first universal folding mobile keyboard), as well as large building projects, and his passion for what is ultimately humane and environmentally sound reaches far beyond this little house.

The name 'L41' is meant to be read as 'all for one', and also suggests the inverse: 'one for all'. The house is intended as a step towards a global housing solution. 'Affordability, mass-production, quality, high design and sustainability is the L41 housing manifesto,' says Katz. And he cites Article 25 of the UN Charter of Human Rights, that 'everyone has the right to a standard of living adequate for the health and wellbeing of himself and his family' as proof that such a solution is not only a delight, it is an imperative. The ability to mass-produce houses, he argues, is crucial to meeting the very basic need for human shelter. Hence the prefabricated design here: the L41 consists of three parts, delivered by flatbed truck, that can be fully assembled in one day.

Yet its high-minded aims are not what first strikes visitors to the L41. Rather, it makes them aware that doing away with excess space is not a barrier to comfort, or even a bit of luxury. Finishes are to a high standard throughout. The kitchen is fitted with high-quality appliances, as Katz felt it was important to spend more on things that would last longer: 'Good-quality appliances with long, low-service lives trump planned obsolescence and appliances in landfills.' The glazed end wall and large living room window open the house to its surroundings, make it feel more spacious and allow for the luxury of unimpeded natural light. Narrower vertical windows at the kitchen end provide some privacy and variation, keeping the interior from feeling like a uniform cube. The external cladding is zinc, chosen for its robustness and low-energy production. The L41 may be a small step towards the global good, but it is a giant leap towards better housing, and yes, it is a delight.

The plan consists of an ample, U-shaped kitchen with a dining bar, a living area that doubles up as a bedroom with pull-out bed, a desk area and a bathroom. There is also a small, covered terrace. The many storage closets and drawers have a streamlined, handleless design, which makes each area feel more spacious.

The walls are constructed with cross-laminated timber, made by pressing sheets of softwood together at right angles to create a 'super-ply' that is both structurally sound and load-bearing, thus eliminating the need for materials that contribute to CO_2 emissions.

The use of CLT could have greater implications for Katz's home province of British Columbia, where an estimated 1 billion cubic metres (35 billion cubic feet) of forest has been killed by pine beetle, and has to be milled in the next decade before it becomes unusable.

FAMILY DYNAMICS

HOUSE LINA
Ulrich Aspetsberger, Caramel Architekten
Linz, Austria
55m² (592 sq ft)

When Ulrich Aspetsberger's wife took a job in a museum in
Linz and came home to Vienna at weekends, it meant that
their young daughter spent a lot of time at home with
her dad. Three years on, the family tired of passing as
commuters, so Aspetsberger, an architect at Caramel
Architekten, came up with a different solution. Since his
parents had a home in Linz with some property attached to
it, he decided to build this 'little house' for his wife and
daughter to use during the week. As a commuter's pied à
terre, it offers an ideal combination of modern efficiency and
homely comforts, especially as the extended family is only
a few metres away across the garden. As a work of small-
scale architecture, it expresses Modernist principles with
a current eye on energy use and environmental awareness.

The first thing that strikes one about House Lina is the
continuous fibreglass cladding in a pleasant shade of yellowy
green, which both blends with the greenery and presents
the house as a standout in an area of more traditional
Austrian suburban style. The colour was a compromise from
something a bit more avant garde, Aspetsberger explains.
He had originally planned to cover the exterior in black rubber,
but his parents, whose bathroom window is mere steps
away from the new house's windowless east façade, were
not so enthusiastic, 'so I chose something more sunny!'

As much as the cladding helps the house to settle into
the garden surroundings, the fully glazed main façade allows
the inhabitants to feel that their environment extends beyond
walls. This aspect was key in the success of such a small
dwelling. 'It was a puzzle to fit in the main functions (sleeping
room, children's room, bath, kitchen), and have a quite

'The inspiration could have been my old VW microbus that I had when I was a student. It was well organized, and gave me a home for many weeks in the summer.'

The structure curves up to enclose the deck, but leaves plenty of room for an array of unusual window openings, so natural light penetrates at many heights and angles. The lightweight construction uses energy-efficient prefabrication methods and thermally robust materials.

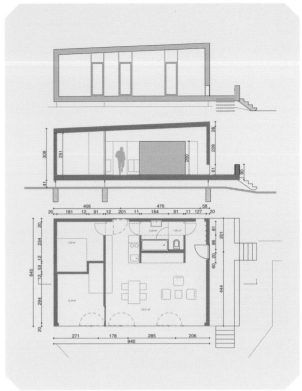

generous living room,' Aspetsberger explains. 'The wonderful garden was a great help. We did not have to close the house to the garden. Instead, the glass façade gives the feeling that the garden is included in the living area.'

The simple, rectilinear structure brings to mind a few Modernist icons, but Aspetsberger says that if he had any model for inspiration, it was the old Volkswagen microbus from his student days. As quirky as the reference may seem, the wraparound wall/roof structure that extends at ground level to create a tidy deck area is slightly reminiscent of the pop-up roof or retractable awning of the iconic VW. Efficiency in layout was matched in the construction, which was accomplished using prefabricated elements that corresponded in size to the dimensions of standard sections of particleboard. Utilizing lightweight construction methods and thermally efficient materials, it took only a few days to

mount the prefabricated elements to the steel framework, which is attached at intervals to a strip foundation.

Though the house needed to fit into the existing plot, there were other reasons for keeping to a minimal scale. Tax liability dictated a house of around 170 cubic metres (6,000 cubic feet), but the small size was also more conducive to the budget. In the end, however, Aspetsberger felt that keeping to a minimum of space made more sense environmentally. He now feels that building on a smaller scale (and with energy-efficient materials) 'is the answer to our global problems. For example, everybody talks about what the energy demands are per square metre, but no one talks about using fewer square metres.' Of course, he says, 'it's much easier to build a bigger house, plus you earn more money on the project, but it is much more satisfying to create something like this'.

The infrastructure is 'docked' onto the existing house, but the house includes all of the requisite services. It was designed to be easily dismounted and moved when necessary. The internal cube structure contains the bathroom and storage with the kitchen on one side. The top of the cube is a play space and guest bed.

The shape and volume of the
basic trailer was retained, and
with an opened-up interior
became a spacious area for
'multifunctional zones' of use.
Katz was keen to maintain an
unobstructed path through the
house from outside to inside,
and out again.

Over a period of two years,
a group of fifty students and
three professors undertook
all aspects of the design,
planning, coordination,
material specification and
reconstruction of the mobile
home. Students worked with
skilled craftsmen and gained
hands-on training, using many
recycled and reclaimed
materials.

UNDER THE MOON

A FOREST FOR A MOON DAZZLER
Benjamin Garcia Saxe
Guanacaste, Costa Rica
68m² (732 sq ft)

It's not hard to admire a well-designed shelter in the lush, unspoiled Costa Rican rainforest. But this house by Benjamin Garcia Saxe shows particular adeptness at respecting the local vernacular, while embracing modern comforts and energy-efficiency. It was the spectacular surroundings that inspired the project, says the architect, who designed and built the house for his mother. 'My mum moved away from the city and built her own home out of tree trunks, mosquito nets and tin,' he explains. 'She placed her bed in a corner to watch the moon as she went to sleep.' Having trained at Brown University and the Rhode Island School of Design, as well as at architecture school in Costa Rica, Garcia Saxe decided to improve on his mother's design, but not her vision of a simple house with a moon view.

The surface simplicity, however, belies a more complex sophistication. The materials are basic – wood and metal, with a concrete foundation – but they have been applied with no small skill. Currently working with Rogers Stirk Harbour and Partners in London, Garcia Saxe has had plenty of experience with larger and more technologically advanced buildings, but he is not inspired to use new technology merely as an end in itself. Rather, he feels that design must keep to the goal of addressing basic desires and needs. His aim, he argues, is to investigate new methods and materials 'as they relate to time and location', and to look at our human desires as a means of creating 'profound new spaces' – hence a house that was built with bamboo cut from a family farm during a full moon (then cured with diesel and dried in the shade), and capped with a corrugated tin roof of a type that has been used in the area for generations. From these

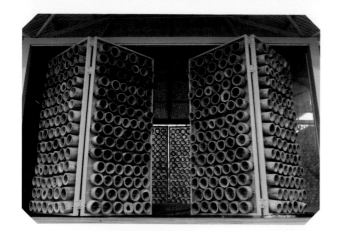

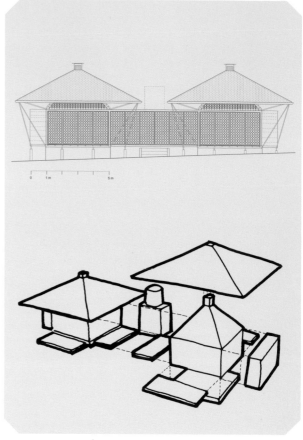

fundamentals, the house explores ideas of enclosure and openness, light and shade, transience and solidity.

Set in a small clearing but surrounded by uncut forest, the house is formed from two modules: one a private bedroom space, and the other a living area. They are joined by an indoor terrace composed of wood decking around a central garden, planted by the architect's mother, and now filled with fan and coconut palms. The two end modules are covered by separate, extended tin roofs that allow for plenty of ventilation. Inside the roof shells, screens made from short lengths of bamboo cuttings create a more enclosed environment, while still allowing for flow of light and air. Similar panels made from cut bamboo are used to create

hinged screens for the large openings on the long elevations. These screens open to wide wood decks that sit partly within the shelter of the roof.

The house's open but structurally robust character is reinforced by the galvanized steel beams and columns that form the frame of the house, and the slender, angled pole supports that join the framework in an elegant and subtle geometry. The new home, Garcia Saxe says, reinterprets his mother's self-made dwelling by providing 'a view to the moon and a very open plan that captures an internal garden, while giving her security when she sleeps'. It also provides a good argument for giving old materials more advanced treatment and allowing simple desires to find extraordinary expression.

Building in his native Costa Rica, Garcia Saxe brought together modern and traditional materials: an efficient steel frame and local bamboo, which was used in a variety of forms. The house is full of neat tricks for encouraging ventilation and natural light, such as the layered roof structure.

PLUS ONE

ONE+ MINIHOUSE
Add-A-Room
Stockholm, Sweden
15m²+ (161 sq ft+)

The idea of modular building has been around for years,
but the concept of reducing it to its lowest footprint with
the highest-quality design is something that the team at
Add-A-Room have brought some much-needed innovation
to. Following on from the traditional Scandinavian
summerhouse concept, and thinking in terms they describe
as a 'Lego system for adults', the designers created a model
that pays homage to tradition, while offering more modern
versatility and ecologically conscious design.

With its dark wood cladding and clean-lined natural
wood interiors, the One+ Minihouse appears to adhere to
a familiar Nordic type, but it makes strides towards even
greater efficiency. The smallest unit measures a mere 15m²
(161 sq ft), small enough to avoid the need for a building
permit in Sweden. Dwellings of this size, called 'friggebod',
are a common sight in colonies of summerhouses, though
some can be nothing more than huts. The One+ Minihouse
contains all the necessary services for a functioning house,
including a petite pergola and deck. But the unit is also
conceived as a 'linking module', which can be added to as
the client wishes, increasing living space or including an
outdoor kitchen through the addition of further connecting
units. This, too, follows on from the Scandinavian tradition of
having a summerhouse that consists of a series of buildings,
but by having linking, rather than stand-alone, units the
One+ Minihouse maximizes energy and spatial efficiency.

Materials and construction are also geared towards
green thinking. The familiar-looking cladding is, in fact, a
relatively new product called 'Superwood', made from a
plentiful softwood – spruce – that has been treated to result

The cladding is a product that uses a plentiful softwood, impregnated with a substance that makes it more durable, akin to hardwood. The units can be used separately, or attached together to create a larger house. Beneath the cladding, thick insulation maintains thermal performance inside.

in a more robust skin, reducing the demand for imported and endangered species of slow-growing hardwood. The glazing is both ample to provide abundant natural light and high-performance to reduce heat loss, while extremely thick insulation helps ensure a comfortable internal temperature, lowering the need for heating (or cooling). The whole unit is prefabricated, again reducing on-site wastage and lowering labour costs, and the house is delivered to site by truck, and then craned into place. It can also be moved when necessary.

The Add-A-Room system was developed by Svenne Hansson, a working carpenter, and his wife Susanne Aarup, who have spent several years running a family business renovating summerhouses in Sweden. The couple teamed up with Danish architect Lars Frank Nielsen, who has made a career injecting sharp minimal design into traditional Scandinavian housing types, as well as in producing public buildings with a crisp, modern sensibility and an underlying warmth in materials. In this design, Nielsen says, 'we wanted to provide an alternative to the existing mini-houses in Sweden that mostly look like playhouses for children'. Their approach, as cute as it may appear, is a sophisticated effort towards minimal living, with every detail carefully mapped to enhance the environment of the single unit or the multi-module house.

It seems a dilemma of our time, the question of how to enjoy the natural environment even as we become increasingly conscious of the impact we have on it. Since we cannot avoid making demands altogether, the answer seems to be to reduce as much as possible, to hone our needs to the minimum. For those who do not wish to compromise the comforts of home, the compact offering of the mini-house seems in many ways an ideal solution. More than a system of highly functional modules, the combination of dark exterior and light internal space, and the inclusion of an outdoor deck area and pergola, add a sense of luxury on a satisfyingly small scale. And the design invites the kind of relaxed, flexible living that too often demands more from the land than from our own ingenuity. Here, the team at Add-A-Room are making a step towards reversing that trend.

2

SMALL
AND
MOBILE

The mobile home as a concept has been around for centuries. Nomadic cultures have long wondered at the necessity of having an abode fixed permanently to one spot, when seasons change and most other animals move along with the weather. Perhaps it is down to our increasingly global view and travel habits, or a harking back to simpler living spaces, but a rethink of mobile units is occurring, and an abundance of inspired new designs have emerged in magazines and across the architecture web in recent years. In these projects, designers have taken up mobility as a prime feature, rather than as a cute amenity. As we become more aware of the environmental impact of everyday living, we have discovered that our house, perhaps our most important possession, could be contributing to the demise of the planet – a discovery that has prompted many of us to question this long-cherished necessity.

Of course, not everyone wants to take up a transient lifestyle. But even for those fond of a home that stays put, there is still appeal in the idea of a shelter that can be moved around to new territory or surroundings. Even the countryside could do without permanent settlements and still allow people to partake of its splendours in situ. That is the idea behind designs like the Fincube (p. 068) by Studio Aisslinger. This house is a much more sleek and luxurious habitation than has ever previously been associated with a movable house, outside a sheik's desert pavilion. All of the elements that are desirable in a fixed abode are present in the Fincube, and still it is designed to make minimal demands on its site and to be moved from place to place.

But careful readers may notice a lack of wheels on the Fincube. Indeed, none of the structures featured in this chapter have wheels: some travel by flatbed truck, or by crane, or both – like the Pod Home (p. 082), designed by students at Ohio State University. Even the most efficient house might be undone environmentally by having to include an engine powerful enough to propel it. This is not a problem for such waterborne projects as Arkiboat (p. 086) by Drew Heath, which uses only small motors suitable for calm waters, or the Silberfisch (p. 064) by Confused-Direction, which needs to be towed to its destination, and the tubular-shaped Roll-It (p. 078), another student-designed project, which takes mobility to a holistic level. The structure includes all of the amenities necessary in a dwelling, but the entire house can be rolled from one site to another.

For Belgian architects dmvA, a mobile unit came about in answer to strict planning regulations that disallowed their designs for a guest house on a client's property. Since the planners couldn't agree with any of their designs for a permanent house, dmvA decided to change categories, from fixed to mobile, from architecture to art (see Blob; p. 058). Even more experimental are Shelter No. 2 (p. 074) by Broissin Architects and the BuBbLe House (p. 090) by MMASA. The former is a panelled, tri-level structure that is quick to assemble and looks like it might leave earth just as quickly, while the BuBbLe House reduces habitable space to the absolute essentials and does a good job of asking the question that many of these projects are trying to answer: just how much space is enough?

ART CIRCUMVENTS PLANNING

BLOB
dmvA Architecten
Antwerp, Belgium
20m² (215 sq ft)

At least the architects cannot be accused of inventing a high-flying philosophical discourse to explain their approach. The young Belgian practice dmvA have won awards for their designs, which include private and social housing, schools, offices and interiors, many of which are rather rectilinear in form. So in this design for a guest house, the designers were also not stamping out a shape that they've tried to employ in variations before. They created something different, for them, and they called it a 'Blob'. They also call it a 'space-egg', but what they won't call it is new.

'The process of design', they argue, 'is not a search for something fundamentally new, but a search for another application for something already existing.' In this case, however, it was mainly the landscape and the many prohibitive regulations that were existing. The shape was created to get around building restrictions that were making it impossible for the team to realize a structure they had been commissioned to design for creative agent Rini van Beek. David Driesen and Tom Verschueren, principals of dmvA, had previously created a cool, modern house extension in the Netherlands for her, an L-shaped block of clear and milky glass with full-height, folding glass doors. The brief here was for something that could be used as an office or as independent guest quarters on Van Beek's property in Belgium. But there was also an existing building to consider: a small, pyramidal wooden summerhouse that was the main residence on the site.

The Blob was designed to sit in harmony with the wooded site, surrounded by tall spruce trees near a lake, and the angular shape of the summerhouse. Making a virtue

'When Blob was presented to the local council...it was immediately rejected. They thought it weird, and it did not fit in with their (rigid) building regulations.'

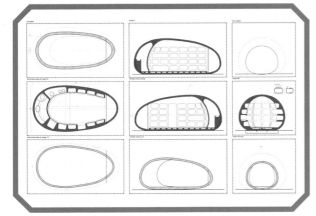

of the planning restrictions, the architects and client decided that something non-permanent was the answer to both the demands of the building regulations and the idea of maintaining the ecological surroundings, which was an important point for everyone. 'It was decided to build something organic', says Van Beek, 'without cutting down a single tree.'

The architects claim that they are 'used to working within limitations, but at the same time eliminating barriers'. So the mobile structure was created to get around the restrictions of a permanent structure, while also providing all of the facilities that the client had asked for. The ovoid shape was made from hand-crafted polyester, which was carefully honed over six months by designer Thomas Denturck of contractors AD&S, who had previously worked with the material in other constructions. It includes a grid of shapes inside that form storage, lounging and sleeping compartments. An isolated bathing space is positioned at one end. The nose of the blob and a side door can be opened to create a sort of open-air pavilion, or it can be closed up to create a sky-lit hermitage.

Kitchen and bathing facilities are all fully functioning, and lighting is set in the recesses of the wall grid or comes through circular floor panels, so that the entire interior space can be left free of furnishings if desired. There are no attached wheels, allowing the unit (roughly the size of a small caravan) to be transported by flatbed truck and then craned into place. It's currently looking for a new home, so it might just turn up to blur some boundaries near you.

With the doors and roof light opened, the Blob appears like an outdoor pavilion. The main house on the property has an unusual triangular shape, which the Blob was meant to complement.

THE SILVER SURFER

SILBERFISCH
Confused-Direction
Oldenburg, Germany
40m² (431 sq ft)

There are boats, there are houseboats, and then there is the Silberfisch, designed by Flo Florian and Sascha Akkermann of Confused-Direction. Without its floating base, this 'silver fish' resembles nothing short of the kind of glamorous loft-style dwelling that would suit the cover of trendy design magazines. The style is slick all right, gleaming white and emphasizing the fact that this is not your average canalside or harbour-tied dwelling. It's a highly civilized but also conscientiously green approach to minimal, transportable living.

Florian and Akkermann have made their name with their range of sensual, organically shaped furnishings and lighting designs, some of which have found a very fitting home in the Silberfisch, helping to underscore a concerted approach to making water dwelling attractive to those enamoured of the high-design lifestyle. But the genesis of the idea for a floating house comes more from what they perceive as global energy and population imperatives. These conditions may mean that the move to occupancy on waterways becomes a real option, in which case, they suggest, their 'open, minimalist design is perfect for the small space'. The idea was not so much to turn a boat used for travel into occasional habitation, but to make 'a houseboat that never leaves the shoreline'. Their solution, they point out, 'has all the beauty and design features that grace many lofts'. It does, and a few more.

Unless you own the penthouse, you aren't likely to get much private outdoor space from a loft building, but the Silberfisch includes both a front 'porch' area and a roof deck, which is accessible from the upper-floor bedroom.

There is also a narrow rear walkway, suitable for standing or sitting for a lazy moment, feet dangling over the side. And while many urban domestic spaces make do with a patch of Astroturf or a few potted plants to provide some greenery, the roof deck here is planted with living grass, a signal of the designers' commitment to the environment and, perhaps, a winking reference to the traditional suburban backyard. (Florian and Akkermann are keen to highlight the idea of 'living on the water in a houseboat with a yard to mow'.) The window opening at the front lights up the main living/kitchen area, making the modest proportions feel like a much larger, lighter space.

Inside, the plan is functional but infused with a bright spark of modern design. Built-in shelves, in the curvy shapes that are a Confused-Direction trademark, line a wall opposite a compact but high-spec kitchen station. The tidy little bathroom is housed towards the rear of this main space, which has a sliding door at the back to allow movement of air and light all the way through. The ladder access to the upper-floor sleeping area might be underwhelming, but the clever insertion of the space with its large, pop-up skylight and access to the top deck is definitely a step towards the wow factor.

But this is no mere glamour palace. The Silberfisch was produced with minimal energy and financial strain: the structure is made almost entirely from wood that was reclaimed from other sources, and without any steel reinforcements. In the future, solar panels will be added to existing energy-saving amenities, which include the green roof, high-performance insulation and a water-saving

'eco-toilet'. There is no motor, as the houseboat is meant to be pulled to its location by kayak (when the wind is low). All of this means that the house produces zero emissions, thus minimizing its already low impact on the planet. Florian and Akkermann admit that the appeal to the general public of living on the water 'might be debatable' at the moment, but there is no question that as the world heads towards a greater need for saving energy and maximizing habitable space, we might think more of a floatable lifestyle.

The houseboat has two floors: the main living space, kitchen and toilet are on the ground floor, while the sleeping area above is accessed by a simple ladder. Another ladder in the sleeping loft leads to the roof deck. The curving, built-in shelves and bowl seat were also designed by the duo.

'The house is a thoroughly modern floating home, which, instead of occupying a valuable plot of land, is anchored in a body of water, allowing residents to remain in a location indefinitely or to relocate on a whim.'

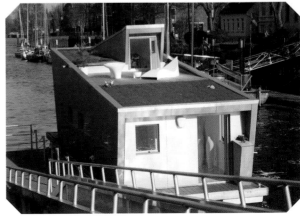

MODERN NOMAD

FINCUBE
Studio Aisslinger
Bozen, Italy
47m² (506 sq ft)

When Werner Aisslinger developed the Loftcube prototype (a mobile living unit that could be airlifted to any usable rooftop site) in 2003, his aim was to create not elite luxury units but communities – specifically communities of people who shared a belief in the values of space, the efficient use of natural resources and the positive potential of human innovation. Aisslinger likened his vision to that of Le Corbusier's vertical habitats, except that the Loftcube would promote 'a sort of cosmic rooftop community'. With the Fincube, Aisslinger is still exploring the possibilities of marrying modern nomadic tendencies with responsible and efficient design. Like the Loftcube, this is a self-contained, mobile unit, but the Fincube can be placed on and hooked into a variety of settings and services. Aisslinger calls this model 'natural high tech', as it has all of the necessary functions controlled by a central touch-panel, while at the same time being made of renewable and recyclable materials.

The Fincube was developed with the help of a South Tyrolean team, who were key in devising and crafting the wood elements. Larch-wood caging envelopes the living block into an organic form that is akin to a woodland mushroom, wrapping the structure horizontally from top to bottom in a warm timber web. The curving larch slats on the exterior also form a screen for the otherwise transparent house, which has floor-to-ceiling triple-glazed window panels on all four sides. Sunlight infuses the house, and the custom-made wood furnishings, though streamlined and modern, take on a natural warmth. The interior structure and finishes are also European larch, except in some instances where the designers chose stone pine for its

pleasant scent. Though it is touted as a nomadic unit, the proportions and facilities are much more slick than your average mobile home, and certainly more luxurious than a yurt. Inside, the living, sleeping, dining and bathing spaces have been finished to a high modern standard. As a prefab product, it can be ordered with or without the bespoke furnishings. And it can be sited virtually anywhere.

As an environmentally friendly concept, the Fincube was designed to make light demands of its surroundings. It requires minimum soil sealing, meaning that the natural soil is only lightly displaced when the Fincube is installed on its four foundation columns. The designers maintain that even this disruption to the natural environment can be easily restored once the Fincube is moved to a new site. The foundation points can also be adjusted to suit the topography, without major carving out or filling of the site. Photovoltaic cells on the roof provide the house's energy needs. As for most mobile living units, however, connections for water, waste water and electricity may be required, depending on the intended use.

Though the idea is that the Fincube could be set in isolation as a low-impact nature retreat, there are still possibilities of a more communal arrangement. The Fincube was developed with South Tyrolean hotelier Josef Innerhofer, with the concept as a vision for hospitality: 'A temporary Fincube village with minimum soil sealing can be placed in the most beautiful landscape without permanently altering them,' says Aisslinger. It's a different kind of community, but one still alert to a sense of wanderlust that calls for shelter that is both substantial and transient.

'The design is minimal, material-oriented and in close touch with nature. It is an answer to the future needs of flexible and smart tourism.'

The 3m- (10 ft-) high interior space is a helical arrangement, with the entrance from a stairway opening onto an open living and dining area. A horizontal ledge surrounds the building and helps screen the 360° of windows.

The original prototype was built 1,200m (3,937 ft) above sea level near Bozen in northern Italy, with the surrounding windows providing a view of the Dolomites.

READY TO LAUNCH

SHELTER NO. 2
Broissin Architects
Tepotzotlán, Mexico
39m² (418 sq ft)

It might resemble a craft that could fly high above the earth, but this modular shelter was actually modelled at a micro-scale, being inspired by the shape of a virus. The house can be used as a stand-alone or as part of a multi-unit housing project. Architect Gerardo Broissin describes his 'Shelter No. 2' as 'an economic, prefabricated, modular dwelling project, designed to be inhabited by two or three people of any socio-economic level'. It is expandable and composed primarily of gypsum products, which are themselves made up of 90 per cent recyclable materials. All and all, it's a small-scale approach to a much larger ambition.

The shape, for all of its geometric distinction, proves very practical for a house on a small scale. A compact, tripartite design allows for more space on the upper floors, while the footprint and roof area (where heat escapes) are kept to a minimum. The wall panels are covered in hexagonal perforations that can all be opened up to allow in natural light, as can the roof panel. This is a key feature of the best micro-designs: letting in enough light and air to make sure that small does not feel cramped, dark or claustrophobic. Broissin's shelter is a magnet for sunlight, which is allowed to penetrate from myriad angles and create layers of light and shadow, not so unlike rays through trees. Inside, the brightness is maintained through the use of white on the walls and for storage, and bold orange furnishings.

Pragmatism is also evident in the sensible arrangement of rooms. While the bottom floor, with its narrow floor space, is restricted to access and the facility for a small, hydroponic garden, the wider middle section accommodates the living room, bath and kitchen with breakfast bar. The top floor makes a fitting aerie for the bedrooms, with sloping walls and reduced ceiling space, reminiscent of many a cosy attic retreat. Efficiency is built into both the construction and the running of the house. A crew of ten or so workmen can assemble the whole from the prefabricated parts in about two days, and appliances are powered by an arrangement of solar panels attached to the surface. Water needs to come from a mains supply, but once it has been used, it is sent through a biological treatment system (also prefabricated) that cleans the water enough for reuse in irrigation.

In addition to its solar system for electrical power, the house has a full array of green credentials. The walls and floors are made from layered panels that sandwich a non-toxic, sustainable insulation (cork) between the layers of gypsum. Double-glazed window panels are made from recycled glass, the bathroom walls are covered in panels made from recycled resin, the structural steel is taken from disused ships, and the furniture is recycled plastic. For the hydroponic wall on the ground floor, the architect devoted a section of the angled wall space to an irrigation system that would allow for gardening without the need for soil.

Not satisfied with designing a successful prototype, Broissin argues that this is a 'real house', capable of housing two adults and a child. He has also created a model for future development, attaching multiple units, virus-like, to a single structure to form an energy-efficient housing block. Broissin adds that Shelter No. 2 has already become 'a detonator of collective and individual ideas' for those who have been able to able to experience it, whether visiting 'for ten minutes or spending a night'.

Though its shape
draws associations
with space travel and
science fiction, the
project's aims are
more earthbound:
to provide a model
for sustainable,
economically viable
housing units.

Walls are panels of fibre-reinforced gypsum boards, made from 90 per cent recycled materials. Windows are recycled double-glazed, high-performance tinted glass, with an air chamber between the layers that improves thermal values. Floors are covered in bamboo panels.

LIFE IN THE ROUND

ROLL-IT
Institut für Entwerfen und Bautechnik
University of Karlsruhe, Germany
2.5 × 3m (6 ft 6 in × 10 ft)

This tubular living space is proof that there is a lot of room for rethinking the standard housing model, especially if we want to scale back our demands. When asked to design a living space that could be moved and set up overnight, then moved on again 'before one has started to annoy the authorities', the creators of the 'Roll-It' took the idea of mobility seriously. But they considered the concept not just in terms of conveyance from one site to another. Mobility is also a key feature of the interior, which, in order to provide all of the basic amenities within a tiny, curved space, is also movable, changeable, flexible.

'Imagine', say the creators of this rolling house, 'that you have to move to another place due to work or study. Instead of looking for a place to live, you bring your own home with you. You could choose a parking space or a nice park to live in. You don't have to ask for permission or a permit.' Well, not until someone wants you to move, which, of course, you can do, with the help of a few strong friends or a flatbed truck. This was the solution presented in a design competition at the University of Karlsruhe by Christian Zwick and Konstantin Jerabek. Roll-It is a highly mobile and totally unconventional design that takes flexibility as a concept from the outside in.

Starting with the structure of a barrel that is 2.5m (6 ft 6 in) in circumference and 3m (10 ft) long, they integrated living, working, sleeping, cooking, bathing and toilet services into the circular interior, and faced them all with friendly, light-grained bent ply. While the designers do not mention any particular inspiration from spacecraft, the highly flexible and non-linear interior recalls the compartmentalized,

spatially inventive living conditions of an anti-gravity interior. Here on earth, however, amenities need to be brought to user level, and some degree of horizontality. So the barrel consists of three service 'rings': at one end is a sleeping/living unit; at the other is the kitchen/washing/toilet hub. In between is the 'corridor', a ring that turns by aid of walking up its slope. Analogies to the hamster wheel are not entirely without reason, since Roll-It was designed to be used for occasional exercise. The ring's more utilitarian function is to help 'dial' the service required for the two end units. The user connects the corridor to one of the two 'furniture shells' on either side, and then walks along until the connected shell is in the desired position. He or she then locks that shell into place until it is necessary to change it again. Dialling the middle corridor also changes the amount of natural light coming into the interior, as windows line up with external openings on the outer layer – or not. It's a lot of flexibility for such a small shell, and a lot of mobility.

The title of the workshop for this project, run by professors Camille Hoffmann and Matthias Michel, was 'Guerilla Housing', an intentionally provocative rubric meant to eschew ideas of conventional shelter. Sadly, it is also a term that highlights the difficulties in creating housing types that defy traditional models, even when they do so in the interest of saving resources and valuable urban space. What the Roll-it really accomplishes, like the best of small-house designs, is a successful enquiry into what is necessary for a comfortable, healthy living space. It also provides a tantalizing glimpse of where such investigations, carried out in earnest and with the fewest preconceptions, might lead.

'Even Diogenes, the first to see himself as both a citizen of the world and the inhabitant of a barrel, would have been amazed at the interior of this particular barrel.'

Services are all fitted within the internal structure. The inhabitant can change access to bed, desk, kitchen or toilet by walking along the centre ring, which can then be locked into place. The structure was made from a specially fabricated plywood.

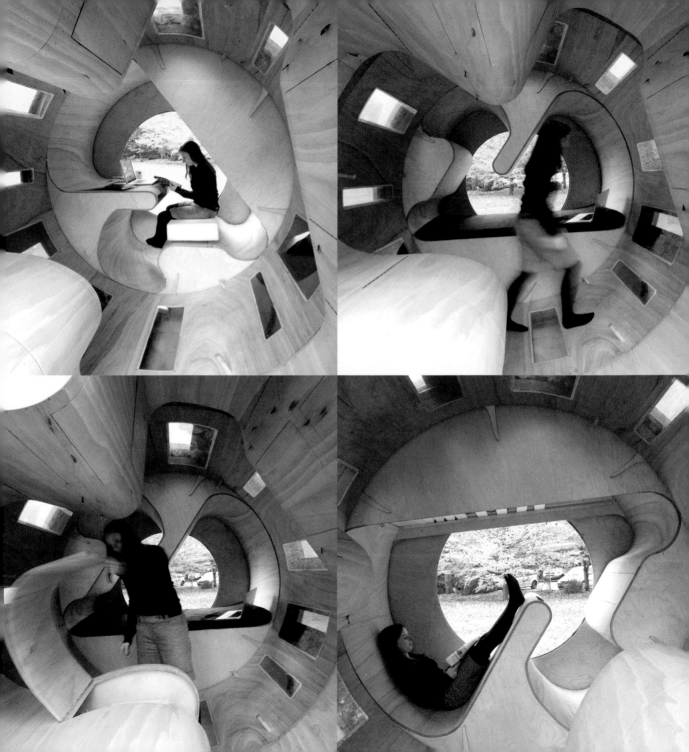

NOT A TOY

POD HOME
Lisa Tilder, Stephen Turk
Ohio State University, USA
12m² (129 sq ft)

The problem with the truly micro-sized house is that it becomes so small as to be considered 'cute' or 'sweet', and therefore not always taken seriously. But the fact that the designers managed to pack so much into so little space is serious indeed, especially when we consider our normal consumption of space and energy by contrast. This bright little 'pod' was conceived by the team at Ohio State University's Knowlton School of Architecture, headed by faculty members and architects Lisa Tilder and Stephen Turk. Like so many of the transformative projects in the Solar Decathlon competition (see chapter 4), the design of the Pod Home was the result of a collaboration between students in the architecture and engineering departments.

At a large university probably best known for its football team (the Buckeyes), the challenge was to reach across campus to make this an interdisciplinary project, and to provide continuity as the schedule ran to three years and some students left, while others joined. Professors Tilder and Turk provided that continuity, and led the team in finding methods to implement the engineering technology into a coherent modern dwelling that would incorporate a package of green energy solutions. These elements have been successfully combined to create a 'flexible living "pod" that could be transported to various sites for a range of needs'.

The most noticeable aspect of the Pod Home, apart from its bright-green colour, is its shape: a distorted trapezoidal volume, which helps to illustrate how the technologies of the house influenced the architecture. The unusual form derived from a series of steps to promote energy efficiency, and from efforts to fit a standard domestic programme into a very tight volume. Beginning with a basic, pitched-roof house, the designers gave one side of the roof a relatively steep angle (55°) to ensure optimum solar-energy absorption by the photovoltaic panels; the east-facing wall was then canted to allow for greater passive-heat gain. Finally, the ridge of the roof was lifted at one end to provide space for a loft bed, accessed by ladder steps. Inside, all of the required services for a domestic dwelling are included, albeit snugly, with a single room for cooking and lounging, and a small bathroom tucked into the corner. The idea here wasn't merely to fit the functions of a typical dwelling into the smallest possible space, but rather 'to explore alternatives to consumer housing, demonstrating...that the average person needs only a small footprint to live comfortably'.

Energy consumption is further reduced by the array of green sources. In using rooftop solar panels to provide electricity and enough glazing for significant passive solar gain, the team employed phase-changing material (PCM) in the flooring. PCM changes from solid to liquid at room temperature, releasing stored energy (heat) in cold temperatures as it solidifies, and storing energy in its liquid state when the air is warmer. The photovoltaic roof panels are arranged in a way that also accommodates a system for heating water. The house is now on display at the Center of Science and Industry, a children's museum in Columbus, Ohio, within its Big Science Park. It has proved a popular attraction, though its real significance in offering viable solutions to less wasteful, more energy-conscious living is indeed far more serious than its bright, tiny, playful appearance might suggest.

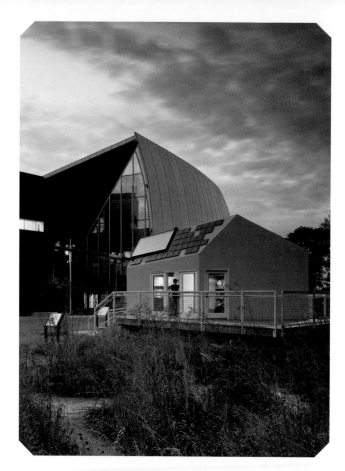

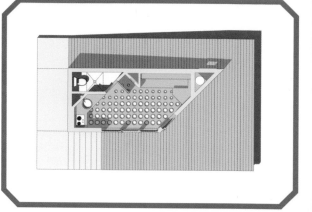

The Pod Home was constructed using locally fabricated panels, which combine structure and insulation to create a high-performance thermal envelope. The interior cladding is FSC-certified plywood.

An antifreeze solution is pumped through the solar collector, where it absorbs energy, and then through a heat exchanger, which transfers the thermal energy from the sun to the hot-water tank.

The custom-designed, digitally fabricated floor houses pockets of phase-changing material, which helps to regulate the internal temperature by storing and releasing heat energy.

PAVILION AHOY

ARKIBOAT
Drew Heath
Sydney, Australia
30m² (323 sq ft)

Houseboats, by and large, do their best to recreate the quotidian comforts of the standard dwelling in compact, waterborne form. Any greater sea-living aspirations are often left to the overreaching desires, and budgets, of the yachting set. For architect Drew Heath, the design of a house for the water deserved a new approach. 'The typical model of a houseboat in this region of Australia', he explains, 'is an extruded box from a pontoon. It has little interaction with the surrounds.' As for outdoor space, something for which modern Australian houses are the envy of those confined to cooler climes, a houseboat's deck space is usually kept to the functional minimum at best.

In his own words, Heath wanted to 'provide a verandah-type deck around a series of vertical planes to be able to open up the interior to the surrounding seascape'. What this amounts to is a clean-lined, Modernist pavilion that floats. Rather than steel and glass, Heath has chosen the singular material of natural wood, which alternates with the sky-, woodland- and lake-view openings that parade around the main space and encourage the sensation of indoor–outdoor expansiveness.

This 'pavilion on water' benefits further from a Modernist sensibility. It is similar, as Heath admits, to many boats in that circulation occurs along the surrounding deck, but here the core 'house' is level with the deck. The effect goes beyond avoiding a change in level: it creates a much more open and free-flowing relationship than on other seagoing homes, which are usually sunk by a few steps, so that the living space becomes a sort of half-basement apartment. Keeping the house well above water level means that the experience of the surroundings is much more immediate, with wind, air and sun permeating all of the spaces.

Though it is set up higher, the pavilion form is still low-lying and rather subtle in the natural context. A generous roof overhang protects the interior from harsh, direct sunlight, and shelters the immediate deck area, contributing, as in most Modernist pavilions, to the indoor–outdoor experience. The smooth, warm-toned wood floor gives continuity to the interior and exterior spaces. Windows and sliding doors mean that the scenery is a constant presence, rather than occasionally glimpsed. The programme is simple, with a living and kitchen area at the front with the steering mechanism, the main sleeping room at the rear, and a small, second bedroom and bathroom in between. Storage is tucked under beds and in built-in units, and the kitchen is kept compact. But the living/kitchen area does have large doors at either side that can be opened fully, making the space feel much grander than its minimal footprint.

Supported on two stainless-steel pontoons and driven by two 25-horsepower motors, the houseboat is lake-worthy, but, admittedly, not made for rough seas. 'Of course, this is no ocean-going houseboat,' Heath says. It was designed to be used in an estuary to the north of Sydney Harbour, 'for quiet, windless and waveless bays'. In such a serene environment, it makes sense to rely on a low-power, simple modern design from which to enjoy the surroundings. A luxury yacht, it is not. It is, however, a rather graceful addition to the landscape.

With its generous roof overhang and floor-level deck, the boat resembles a Modernist pavilion in the International Style. Walls and beams are of lightweight timber, and plywood was used to form box beams and bracing walls. The roof is a composite of metal sheeting and foam panel.

'The scale of the spaces is quite generous in houseboat terms, although it is small for a typical house.'

FILLING IN THE GAPS

BUBBLE HOUSE
MMASA Arquitectos
A Coruña, Spain
4m² (43 sq ft)

It has come to the attention of some of the more experimental architects that the space needed to accommodate a growing, often transient, urban population is to be found between, around, even on top of, the existing infrastructure. Studio Aisslinger's Loftcube, designed to sit atop a building, Stefan Eberstadt's Rucksack House, which can be hung off the façade, and Richard Horden's MicroCompact home, made to fit happily anywhere extra accommodation might be needed, all speak to the desire to provide self-contained shelter without making permanent demands on the site. Since most cities are already brimming with large, monolithic buildings that crowd out natural light and open space, what is the point of adding even more steel and glass, bricks and mortar? This is precisely the question that Luciano Alfaya and Patricia Muñiz of MMASA address with their BuBbLe construction. 'The core argument', they say, 'is the appropriateness of creating temporary residential spaces in contemporary cities, thus learning the value of ephemeral, dynamic and flexible elements.'

So where many might see a plastic tent, Alfaya and Muñiz see a potential to shelter people in the areas they call 'the cracks of programmed elements', or 'urban voids'. Their point is that even within those programmed areas, there is still room for flexibility, and that even underused private spaces might be exploited in this way. Their solution is this transportable, easy-to-assemble, low-cost kit shelter, which addresses 'four basic problems that have not been solved by conventional temporary structures: to be uniform in height along the entire surface; to have a cover that provides insulation and comfort and can be adapted to

specific circumstances; to have a solid structure that ensures rigidity; and to provide basic hygienic services.'

The entire 'building' fits into a metal carrying box that becomes a block of services for the house, containing a sink and a cooker. A series of metal poles are fitted together to form the structural frame, then a single piece of double-layered plastic is stretched across it to form the walls and roof. Another piece of plastic covers the floor, and there is an inflatable bed. A solar panel supplies energy for lighting and light electrical devices. So far, so tent-like. The real innovation is in the double-layered membrane that is sealed at intervals to form a series of different-sized pockets, or 'bubbles', which can be used as storage, for clothing or other soft articles that then act as insulation for the shelter. A picturesque rendering shows the bubbles filled with

leaves, providing privacy and a salubrious green backdrop. The bubbles can also be used to store water for use by the occupants, which, the architects surmise, could be obtained from a public fountain. Making the plastic envelope from a single sheet helps with ease of installation and contributes to the thermal condition inside. An external shower and chemical toilet can be added for longer stays.

The bare-bones lifestyle required to live in such a sparse shelter is not for everyone, and there is a certain student-style radicalism in this approach, but the underlying premise cannot be easily sidelined. Especially with so many cities struggling to produce adequate housing for their financially challenged numbers, the time to test our flexibility with regard to the concept of shelter in urban spaces might be at hand.

The walls and roof are made from a single sheet of double-walled plastic, with sealed sections that can be filled with clothing or other items for storage (and insulation), as well as water for domestic use.

3

MICRO-
RETREATS

Ah, the appeal of a cosy cottage in the woods, a lovely little lair surrounded by trees and blue sky. This is the kind of small house that most people can relate to and admire without questioning size. It might seem somewhat unfair to reach for the rural retreat as a solution to the challenge of downsizing our living space – after all, a house used for a restful weekend or a few weeks' holiday does not need to cater to the spatial demands of everyday life – but these examples from Chile and Korea, Canada and Australia, France and the Netherlands, Sweden, Taiwan and the US offer more than just a pretty hideaway. The array of small spaces are as different stylistically and programmatically as they are disparate geographically. The idea that these houses are only suited for temporary habitation has, in most cases, more to do with their remote location and availability of services than with any inherent lack of livability or, indeed, any compromise in materials or design – areas in which ingenuity is greater than the measure of the floor space.

The rural cabin is ripe for taking ideas for compact living, but the few included here merit attention for much more than their small size. Taylor Smyth's take on the Canadian 'bunkie' (p. 118) is certainly an exercise in reduction. In this case, the cabin does not possess the full range of services (running water or cooking facilities), but this delicately wrought, timber-slatted sleeping cabin and porch offers a shining example of possibilities. At only 25.5m² (274 sq ft), it could easily be extended for year-round use and still have a footprint that is well under the limit of 75m² (807 sq ft) set for this book. And the quality of

space, material and light would still better than in most larger dwellings. Another example of a cabin pared down to essentials but still overflowing with sensory experience is Stephen Atkinson's mountain hideaway in Colorado (p. 106). This is a complete house with all of the services, but it wears them like a close-fitting coat. The style is less rustic than Taylor Smyth's sleeping space, but it has a quiet modernity that is built to accommodate, rather than challenge, the site.

In the French countryside, Cyril Brulé's Cabanon (p. 110) makes a direct connection with Le Corbusier's iconic hut, but – unlike the master's – is also concerned with its place within the context of the existing rural architecture. Similarly, a guest house in the Chilean mountains (p. 096) was designed to sit within the folds of the hillside and appears as a gentle insertion, the mixed-straw wallcovering visible beneath polycarbonate cladding. Settling even further into the ground are the peaceful spaces of Byoung Soo Cho's underground house (p. 124), inspired by a poet whose own inspiration drew from the earth, air and stars. Also directly in tune with nature is the Chen House in Taiwan (p. 114), by Marco Casagrande. Its design was determined by the very strong typhoons that are common in the area, and the architect's great hope is for the building to become a ruin – 'when the manmade has become part of nature'. Paan Architects' Holiday House (p. 128) in Sweden is unlikely to succumb to nature anytime soon, being clad in sheet iron, but its profile, sitting deliberately low into the hilly ground, makes it another example of a discreet haven whose interior, though not grand, is generously welcoming.

BY INVITATION ONLY

CASA INVITADOS
AATA Arquitectos
Licancheu, Chile
26m² (280 sq ft)

The task was to design a small cabin for trips to the countryside. It only needed the basic amenities, therefore, but the project was also meant to result in a low-energy dwelling that could withstand rough weather and an exposed position on the hillside. So special care was taken with the orientation, the insulation, the window positioning and, of course, the building materials. These are modest aims for a structure that has turned out to have such a remarkable appeal. The simple form peeking out from the greenery of the mountain setting does make an inviting prospect. Closer inspection reveals more intriguing elements, but all still contained within a pleasing simplicity.

The structure is a 540cm (213 in) cube, constructed of timber and containing two levels. The walls were then covered, or built up, with straw bales mixed with stucco and mud, which provides great thermal efficiency when temperatures change dramatically from winter to summer. The mixture is then shielded from the rain by sheets of transparent polycarbonate. Hard-wearing zinc is used at the top and bottom margins of the plastic sheets, providing a material grounding for the building, a satisfying solidity that is also found in the use of local wood for the interiors. The roof is a green solution that has been laid with the same soil/vegetation as local pasture – a solution that protects the structure from both wind and heat. The architects say they consider the roof not as an unseen necessity, but as a fifth façade, since it is so important to the house's thermal environment and because it is visible from certain angles.

Large openings at the front give the house the feeling of a summer pavilion, though it can be secured in cold weather, and also allow for the greatest penetration of winter sunlight for passive heating inside. Windows on other walls are smaller, but positioned to allow for effective ventilation in warm weather. The interior was painted white to maximize the effect of natural light indoors and reduce the need for artificial lighting. The floor plan is also satisfyingly simple: an open living space, kitchen and bathroom occupy the ground floor, while the upper floor is a loft-style sleeping area. The architects chose the two-level plan, rather than a bungalow, to minimize the disturbance of the site. The use of natural solid timber with the whitewashed finish makes for a clean interior with a feeling of modernity that is still comfortably rustic.

It would be easy to dismiss such a basic design as a mere function of shelter. But the various elements of materials and surfaces demonstrate that this is a project that has turned a small amount of built space into an environmentally conscious structure that also provides more than adequate shelter. It's a thing of simplicity, but that simplicity has been well honed, taking inspiration from a rugged landscape and a vast perspective. Guests will feel honoured indeed to find their way here.

In accordance with the house's low-energy requirements, the interior was painted white to bounce natural light off the walls and reduce the need for artificial light, and the windows were positioned to allow for plenty of sunlight in winter and a cross-flow of air in summer. The straw-and-mud stucco wall material is visible through the polycarbonate cladding. The top and bottom margins are finished in zinc.

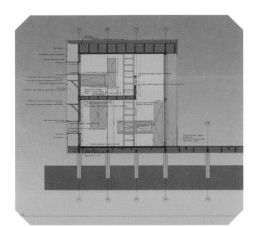

CIRCLING THE ISSUE

MERRY-GO-ROUND HOUSE
Bureau Ira Koers
Drenthe, Netherlands
55m² (592 sq ft)

Medieval builders gave us the great hall for communal gathering, eating and shelter. Later on, rooms were partitioned for separate uses, and the hall became a gallery for both promenading and exhibiting one's collection of paintings and sculpture. In the 20th century, the hall became more of a conduit, serving mainly to access a series of rooms that were closed off for easier heating. In Ira Koers's view, the typology of the house – particularly the holiday cottage – has been too static for too long. 'The design of the Merry-Go-Round gives new meaning to the holiday cottage', she says, 'by taking the traditional floor plan with its rooms opening onto a central hallway and turning it inside out.' So rather than having a hallway that leads into a house, here the access corridor runs around the perimeter, with all rooms open to this continuous walkway. It is a little like walking around a carousel and choosing a horse to ride, hence the name. But it is also more intriguing, like a maze, with the bathroom – reached through a narrow, tiled space between the two sleeping alcoves, and around the back of the kitchen – being the only really enclosed room, its skylight marking the centre point of the scheme.

There are eight alcoves in all set within the square plan. The two sleeping areas are bed alcoves with a platform structure that contains storage underneath and a mattress on top. Around the corner is a small sofa tucked a little ways into the wall, and farther along is the living area, or 'sitting suite', with its built in, U-shaped sofa lining the three internal walls, facing outward, as do all of the rooms, towards the natural landscape. (It also has a wall-mounted television in case visitors crave other stimulation.) Around

the next corner is a block of storage and the dining area, which, taking up a corner position, has two walls that can be left open for a more expansive feeling. There is a built-in bench and rather generous table, but instead of the vivid pinks and reds of the sitting suite, these are made from warm wood and wood veneer. Next to the dining space, a small galley kitchen follows the wall (the bathroom is on the other side), and then the next corner brings us back to the sleeping areas with the bathroom corridor between them.

It feels like a game of hide and seek, following along and finding the various rooms cleverly pocketed into the cube. Or it's as if the living core of Mies van der Rohe's Farnsworth House had been expanded nearly to the boundary of the glazing, so that walking the perimeter became a journey within, rather than without. But Koers has taken more care with privacy and protection than Mies thought necessary. The Merry-Go-Round house is clad in eighty-eight panels, forty-four of which are shutters with glazing behind them. From the outside the panels appear green; from the inside, white. When all the shutters are open, they cover the fixed panels and the building transforms from green to white, with forty-four vertical windows. When they are all closed, the house becomes a softly hued monolith in the forest, the colour harmonizing with the verdant surroundings.

Built as part of an art programme to develop new possibilities for the holiday-cottage typology, the Merry-Go-Round house is a one-off, permanently sited holiday home. But as a concept, it opens many doors, not to mention perspectives, on the form as well as the potential of the small house in the landscape.

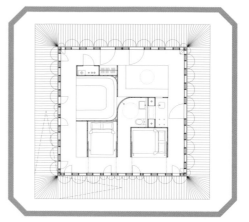

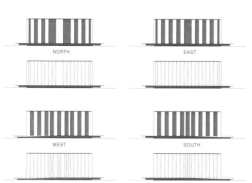

NORTH

EAST

WEST

SOUTH

All functions are set around the perimeter in eight open alcoves, with the shower area at the core beneath a central skylight. 'Furniture, colour, light, material, lines of sight and views', notes Koers, 'are all bundled into one compact, fixed interior.'

The façade has eighty-eight
panels, of which forty-four
are shutters with glass behind
them. The panels are painted
green on the outside and
white on the inside. When the
shutters are open, they cover
the fixed panels so that the
colour changes from green
to white. There are fifteen
opening door/windows.

HIGH MODERN

VACATION CABIN
Stephen Atkinson Architecture
Durango, Colorado, USA
27m² (291 sq ft)

It's not your average nature hut. This vacation house has the earmarks of a rustic retreat: it is surrounded by dense woodland, 2,286m (7,500 ft) above sea level, with a view across a wide river valley in southwestern Colorado, a place known for its rugged mountain landscape. And it's the size of a small outpost, containing all the basic necessities in a minimal shelter.

But the brief was for something that was 'not a log cabin', a building that was sustainable in its construction and operation, fire-resistant, and perhaps something else less tangible. The plan takes a 7 × 7m (24 × 24 ft) square and devotes half to interior living/sleeping/bathing space, and half to a covered deck. This creates 'a yin and yang balance of exterior and interior spaces', the architects say, with the recessed base increasing its 'iconic, even aloof presence'. The two entrances at either end of the porch were also meant to 'counterbalance any traditional central symmetry'. Another contributor to the cabin's aloofness in the landscape is the use of materials. Rather than displaying log or clapboard cladding, the house is finished with non-combustible plaster stucco, a metal roof and metal fire shutters. These elements are obviously practical answers to concerns about brush fires, but their use on such a low-lying rectilinear form speak of contemporary design solutions, a new modernism sitting with cool composure in a place of elemental beauty.

The house feels very much like a protective shelter. The double-sized overhang of the roof creates a low-horizontal front porch, with wide-plank decking orientated across the plan towards stone-lined footpaths at either side, so that

entering the cabin means crossing a vista obstructed by a trio of slim vertical supports. Two sets of sliding glass doors at either side of the centre face towards this view. At the back of the house, in the direction of the approach, a bank of eight top-hung windows sit just above the middle height, making the interior a lot brighter than its solid-seeming shape would lead you to suspect.

Though the architects and client eschewed traditional wood and rustic styles, they adhered closely to a scheme of sustainability. The design, say the architects, 'utilizes sustainable construction materials and local suppliers whenever possible'. The wood framing and plywood were all from sustainably harvested lumber. Paints and finishes are low VOC, the external render is lime-based, and the bath area is finished in mud plaster. A concrete counter was locally made, and the carpentry and furniture were milled and constructed from trees found dead on the site or felled during the insertion of an entry road. Insulation is from a soy-based spray urethane and shredded, recycled denim. These aspects are mostly hidden, but strike an important note of awareness.

With an office based in Northern California, Stephen Atkinson has produced small-house and cabin designs in many parts of the US, and has a particular way with 'new vernacular' designs that pay tribute to traditional building types, while employing the best and most efficient practices of modern building. Here, he has created a shelter that is posed as a new form in an old landscape, but which, perhaps because of its diminutive size, speaks quietly of modern design with an environmental conscience.

The cabin features a non-combustible exterior, together with a metal roof and shutters, to increase its fire-resistance. Though the exterior appears more modern than most country cabins, the materials are eco-friendly and were generally sourced locally. The plan is half interior space and half outdoor deck, facing the expansive view.

ALL ABOUT THE LAND

LE CABANON
Cyril Brulé, Atelier Correia
Villiers-en-Morvan, France
20m² (215 sq ft)

The small cabin that Cyril Brulé designed and built for himself
in a rural village in Burgundy is an exercise in reduction.
It was designed in his studio, and then re-assembled in
about sixty days on a plot of land among some outbuildings
on a former dairy farm. The idea was to reduce living space
to the minimum, and to make the most of the outdoors. The
hills, the field and all the green landscape beyond are meant
to be part of the experience of a structure that Brulé
describes as neither cottage nor mobile home, hut nor
shack. It can be lived in, but it's not meant to encompass
all of life, which is meant to be experienced beyond the four
walls. It's the intimate pleasure of a small shelter that Brulé
celebrates inside, even while constantly pointing, figuratively
at least, to the outdoors.

This is not to say that the architect hasn't given thought
to materials, structure, openings and, of course, position,
for all of these decisions contribute to the studied simplicity
of the 'cabanon'. One recalls the similarly named structure
that Le Corbusier designed as a holiday hut for himself and
his wife on the Côte d'Azur, but Le Corbusier's structure is
much more rough-hewn on the outside and finely kitted out
on the inside than Brulé's edition. The former used a lot of
ply, but the interior has a lovely golden wood veneer on the
many sliding and folding doors and furnishings, and lively
coloured wall paintings. As the ideal getaway for the master
of the concrete tower, Le Corbusier's cabanon could be
seen as a contradiction, if the attention to light, space and
proportion weren't so obvious. He called it 'my castle on
the French Riviera', and given his penchant for overturning
expectations, the castle reference is not so surprising.

Neither cottage nor mobile home: Le Cabanon is an ultra-simple shape that functions as both home and office for the architect. Details include siding made from Nordic fir, duck-feather insulation and an interior lined with formaldehyde-free OSB panels.

Brulé's version is constructed mainly from Nordic fir and sits on a concrete base, but is slightly elevated, some 60cm (24 in) from the ground, so that it hovers in the grass. The shape and materials are indeed very basic. Sheets of modest oriented strand board (OSB) cover the walls inside. Fixtures are made from stainless steel and the ceiling from plain wood planks, but, as with most noteworthy designs, the way these materials are employed takes simplicity to an art. The windows are different shapes and sizes to make the interior more varied, with narrow horizontal openings over the little workstation, an oversized entrance that gives a grand view of the landscape, and smaller box windows at other elevations. The shape is not actually a regular square, but a trapezoidal form that opens out to the glazed entrance, which presents itself to the rolling landscape.

Brulé's grandest claims for his little wooden retreat have nothing to do with its more famous antecedent. Rather, they are that the little building makes the landscape the dominant presence in the life of the inhabitant, that it fits in with the cluster of outbuildings surrounding the main house of the farm, and that it is 'clearly intelligible', being a small, wood construction that offers warmth and shelter from the open countryside and makes few demands of the intellect or view beyond that. It's not trying to teach us anything about building philosophies, except that a very simple, considerate approach, well executed, can produce a very satisfying piece of architecture.

7.6

3.6

2 m

To preserve the ground space, the building is raised on six concrete pilots. The house sits within the grounds of a former dairy and cattle farm. It was built in a carpenter's workshop and then transported to the site, where the main structure was reassembled in about sixty days.

HOUSE OF WIND AND WATER

<u>CHEN HOUSE</u>
Casagrande Laboratory
Sanjhih, Taipei, Taiwan
62.5m² (667 sq ft)

'With this house', says Finnish architect Marco Casagrande, 'we were looking forward to designing a ruin.' The statement isn't meant to prophecy the destruction of the building, but to play with definitions, to provoke an understanding of the project as an unobstructive part of the landscape. When Casagrande further explains his belief that 'a ruin is when the manmade has become part of nature', it becomes clear that the word has taken on a more positive meaning. It is this more holistic view of man in nature that has inspired the design of a minimal hut set within the grounds of a Japanese cherry farm in the Datun mountains of northern Taiwan.

But the idea that the structure is wholly subservient to its surroundings belies the sheer elegance and thoughtfulness of the scheme. 'It is designed as a vessel to react to the demanding wind, flooding and heat conditions of the site,' says Casagrande, and to this end a number of practical steps have been employed. The spaced wood cladding and large openings permit the strongest wind to sweep through the house, rather than butt against it. Gentler breezes ventilate the rooms on hot days, picking up refreshing moisture from the nearby freshwater reservoir pond that sits between the site of the house and the neighbouring farmlands. The structure is raised off the ground, sitting on short sections of concrete pipe in order to allow water to run underneath during periods of flooding.

The basic and very open design makes the building seem more like a rough shelter than a permanent house, but still there is refinement here. The strong horizontality of the house, with its extended outdoor deck, stretches almost to a vanishing point towards the mountains. Its low form makes it less wind

'The tilted roof terrace feels like a landing strip on an aircraft carrier, sending people off to the jungle.'

The structure was designed to withstand typhoons, with a raised floor that allows for occasional flooding. This 'bioclimatic architecture' is also designed to catch the breeze from the Datun River and a nearby reservoir on hot days. The living area includes a fireplace, also used for cooking. A small bathroom with a sauna is set off to one side.

resistant, but also an elegant shape on the flat land. The arrangement allows for flexible movement between the indoor and outdoor spaces, while the small bathroom and kitchen section act as ballast, stabilizing the wood structure during the frequent typhoons. These are located in a volume that protrudes from the eastern elevation, an anchoring arrangement that includes a sauna off of the bathroom. Casagrande explains that the impact of nature is not just a poetic conceit. 'There are typhoons, seven to ten each year, and earthquakes,' he says. And then there is the 'dragon wind', which 'shoots straight from the cold mountaintop to a hot spot down below. It happened during the construction period, when the ground was not yet cultivated. The wind took down our scaffoldings, even bending the steel tubes.' Mrs Lee, a local octogenarian, advised the builders to cultivate the land, and so cool the ground before building. 'We started gardening immediately,' Casagrande says, and it did seem to help. Mrs Lee offered further advice: 'She told us to get geese to keep the snakes out.'

There is a brickwork fireplace for use during the winter months set in the middle of the open living space (rather than against an external wall) to provide maximum heat through the house. A roof terrace is accessed by a stair of the same wood. It slants upward, with high walls at one end and no barrier at the other, only a clear view of the jungle. The chimney, which pierces the roof, is low, so that it can be used for smoking and grilling food.

Built mainly of mahogany, the house has a very elemental quality, especially as the hue has an affinity with the reddish soil that predominates in the immediate area, where vegetation is sparse. But the architect argues that 'the house is not strong or heavy – it is weak and flexible'. While designed to give the farmers some necessary shelter, Casagrande points out, 'it is not about closing out the environment'. Such a permeable design never could close out much of the world, but its virtue lies in the fact that, rather than defying the natural elements, it seems almost to welcome them, while offering robust protection with a lightness of touch.

LAKE LIGHT

SUNSET CABIN

Taylor Smyth Architects
Lake Simcoe, Ontario, Canada
25.5m² (274 sq ft)

This little lakeside dwelling lives up to its romantic-sounding name, as the louvred windows filter in streams of sundown rays and glimmering twilight. Architect Michael Taylor describes the one-room house as 'a simple but sophisticated Canadian bunkie', referring to the traditional small cabins, or bunkhouses, that are common in the region and can often nowadays be built from kits of parts. Set on a rocky outcropping on a slope on the southern shore of Lake Simcoe, the cabin makes few claims on the landscape, but offers inhabitants both warming shelter and a vivid experience of the forested surroundings. It also provides privacy and a nice piece of modern design.

For the architect, the structure evokes 'the "primitive hut" of branches constructed in the wilderness'. It does this by being open, with glazing on three sides, softly screened by a skin of cedar slats. This patterned skin is punctured by intermittent horizontal gaps and larger openings that vary the rhythm of the timber elements, and allow light to play across the interior without forsaking privacy. In winter, the sharp horizontality of the slats contrasts, as Taylor notes, 'with the vertical rhythm of the bare tree trunks'. They also create a dynamic sightline out to the limpid plane of the lake, which shimmers in close proximity to the house.

Though the thoughtful design belies comparisons with the rustic bunkie, the construction was engineered to be as straightforward as possible, given the challenges of the outlying location and the rugged terrain. The structure is made up of prefabricated sections set on two steel beams, which in turn sit on top of concrete caissons. In order to simplify the building process, the whole thing was

prefabricated in a parking lot over a period of four weeks. The components were then numbered, and the structure disassembled and transported to the site, where it was reconstructed in only ten days. Once built, it was given a 'green roof', planted with sedum and herbs, which, in addition to providing insulation and rainwater absorption, helps to camouflage the little hut.

One of the cabin's great achievements is the way it is attuned to seasonal changes. In spring, its delicate exterior blends easily with the vegetation, while in winter the low-lying form helps it hug the snow-covered landscape. Night and day also make their own mark, with the sun casting patterns of light and shadow, and the darkness of rural night allowing the cabin to display what the architects call 'its lantern-like quality, radiating golden electric light from between the slats'. The cabin was not built as a functioning house. The clients have a main home further up the hill, but wanted 'a private retreat that would enhance their enjoyment of the landscape in a spot where they had always watched the sunset'. So the structure includes an open sleeping space, with a wood-burning stove for heat. There is a composting toilet, and an outdoor shower and sink are fed by water from the lake in summer. Though there are no plans to make this a fully equipped living space, there is plenty here to inspire nature-loving designers towards achieving a little romance and compact efficiency.

'Nestled into a slope on the southern shore of Lake Simcoe, this one-room sleeping cabin is a simple but sophisticated Canadian bunkie.'

The wood-and-glass box of the Sunset Cabin hovers lightly above the lake shore. The walls are composed entirely of glass, augmented with an exterior horizontal cedar screen that both braces the structure from twisting and filters the bright summer sunshine.

The interior surfaces are fabricated of birch veneer plywood. The controlled patchwork of horizontal louvres creates a pattern of light and shadow across the interior that changes throughout the day. A small porch faces onto the lake.

Minimal furnishings include a bed with built-in drawers, a wall of storage cabinets and a wood-burning stove. In winter, natural light warms the spare interior; in spring, shade comes with the onset of new growth.

EARTHLY DIGNITY

<u>EARTH HOUSE</u>
BCHO Architects
Gyeonggi-do, South Korea
32.5m² (344 sq ft)

It has the austere grace of a monk's cell and the rigorous
geometry of a Modernist icon. In a forested area in the
Gyeonggi province, located in the northeast corner of South
Korea, Byoung Soo Cho of BCHO Architects has built a house
for meditation and relaxation, and set it 2.7m (7 ft) below
ground – the depth, Cho says, is 'somewhere between
comfortable and uncomfortable'. In some ways, this house can
be seen as one more in a series of the architect's experiments
with fundamental materials and invisible support.

 Cho had used PC cable in his two-storey concrete Four
Box House (2007) to free the structure of columns; in the
Two Box House (2005), he used embedded steel plates,
which he explains, helped to achieve the industrial feeling
that the clients desired. But those plates also formed part
of a continuous structural envelope that did away with any
extraneous elements, leaving only an elemental purity. In
these and the Concrete Box House (2004), Cho had made
the raw concrete volume a thing of both monumental solidity
and earthly grounding. In Cho's work, what appears to be
a dense, fortress-like cube of solid concrete often reveals a
hidden courtyard arrangement inside, with all of the internal
rooms facing a light, open, tranquil space. In some schemes,
long, horizontal windows at ground level link the interior to
the outdoors and very immediately to the site.

 The Earth House has this same essential integrity. It's
as if one of Cho's graceful solid forms has sunk itself into
the very earth below. Here, another nearly hidden courtyard
opens the building to the sky, but at the level that should
delineate the ground-floor space. This act of prompting an
upward gaze is part of the lyricism of the building, which

ON THE ARCHIPELAGO

<u>HOLIDAY HOUSE</u>
Paan Architects
Väto, Sweden
42m² (452 sq ft)

It could be easy to dismiss this house as an unrealistic living space. It is a holiday retreat, after all, set in the grounds of a larger farmhouse and used to accommodate guests and family who do not wish to share quarters in the main house. However, this dark little satellite is a fully equipped house that could as well function as a year-round home. Perhaps it is the way the architects have set the structure low into the landscape, using the dark exterior and an angled form to retreat into, rather than break out onto, the terrain that makes it seem less substantial than it really is. The little structure was designed to yield to 'the diversity of its immediate physical surroundings (meadow, water, garden)', say Maria Papafigou and Johan Annerherd of the young Athens-based firm, Paan. So it is sunk deeper than the main building or the road, and 'folds back to become part of the landscape'. The shape, they say, was inspired by the natural setting. The use of a single, dark-coloured material on the exterior was a further step towards minimizing the visual impact.

But while the structure was meant to be unobtrusive from the outside, the architects worked to maximize the experience from the inside. The angle of the two small wings allows for a sheltered, private deck outside the living space, from where the residents can enjoy an uninterrupted view of the archipelago and the sea beyond. The arrangement of kitchen, sitting room, bedroom and bathroom is basic yet highly efficient, leaving as much room as possible for flexible living space. A 'functional wall' contains the kitchenette and storage space, leaving precious floor space uncluttered with further furnishings. It also hides a two bunk beds within the built-in sofa/niche.

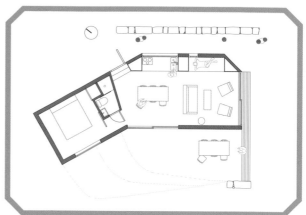

The interior takes in as much natural light as possible through ample windows and sliding doors sited on the 'private' side of the house. Storage, two-tier bed/seating and kitchen units line one wall, leaving more open floor space for flexible arrangements.

Construction work was similarly efficient, as the wood frame was prefabricated and assembled on site in just one day. This was then clad in black sheet iron, an unusual choice for a country where traditional houses are clad in wood, often painted red. According to the architects, the material is more often used for roofing, but its use here ties the building to the local vernacular, while maintaining a new approach to the design. It also allowed them to take advantage of the expertise of local builders, who are used to working with the sheet iron – although perhaps not in precisely the same way.

Energy demands are kept to a minimum. Thick insulation and careful orientation with regard to sun and wind help to maintain a comfortable constant temperature indoors during both summer and winter. A wood-burning stove is also used for heating, and during warmer months natural cross-ventilation is encouraged by the window placement. According to the residents, 'you only need a small house in the summer, since the weather is normally good and the light and long summer nights invite outdoor life'. But they also feel that the house works well in winter, 'when you need a house that can be warmed up quickly and economically'.

Though the little cottage is on the grounds of a 1905 farmhouse, and its form allows it to settle quietly into the countryside, it was also meant to be marked out as a modern addition. 'The fact that we built it in present times should be obvious,' say the family, as it provides 'the daily aesthetic pleasure of good design'. This, in the end, is what Paan delivered, low-impact and high-calibre new architecture that still shows some reverence for what came before.

So as to sit quietly in the landscape, the house is sunk deeper than other structures nearby. Its angled, longitudinal form also reduces its visual impact. The exterior cladding appears as dark-painted wood, but is actually black sheet iron, a robust material commonly used for roofing in the area.

OFF-GRID IN THE OUTBACK

<u>BATH HOUSE</u>
Craig Chatman, ARKit
Collingwood, Victoria, Australia
Less than 50m² (538 sq ft)

As popular as prefabricated buildings have become in the last decade or so, there is still a lot of room for innovation, as Craig Chatman demonstrates with his elegant 'Bath House', so-called for the inclusion of a sauna in one of its two pavilions. It is, Chatman says, 'a great experience on a cold night after finishing a sauna to dash across the deck, knowing another warm room awaits you'. This, in a nutshell, is the wonder of a place that extends beyond its energy-efficient, cost-effective construction. There is a sauna, there is a deck, there is another warm living space – all contained in a footprint of less than 50m² (538 sq ft). The two near-cubic structures, clad in Western red cedar, appear to mirror one another across a wood-lined outdoor space. Call them boxes if you must, but these are high-performances boxes, full of comfort and trim-line design, the cladding softened by being layered in columns that, from a distance, have the delicate quality of a far less sturdy material.

It's a seemingly simple recipe, but one that took the architect five years of research to produce. After setting up his own firm, following his studies at the Royal Melbourne Institute of Technology, Chatman became interested in the idea of prefabrication. It was a means of diversifying his practice, but he was also interested for reasons that have brought so many architects around to prefab design in the last decade: the aspects of affordability, the achievements possible in sustainability, and the involvement an architect has in the manufacturing process. It was the production of the panel system, which Chatman eventually decided to use, that took so much time in development. 'During my initial research,' he explains, 'I was surprised that nobody

The function of the deck is 'to take advantage of the distant views, particularly the Grampians National Park, and to function as an observation deck from which to view the local wildlife'.

Wall panels are made from Western red cedar cladding on insulated, timber-framed panels. Internal wall lining is premium-grade ply.

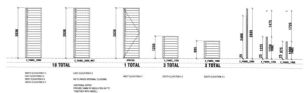

PANEL SCHEDULE

(in Australia, at least) was involved in a panellized approach to the design of a complete façade/cladding system.' By keeping the production in one factory under the supervision of the architect, the panels could be produced much more efficiently, especially when they adhered to industry-standard sizes. Waste is minimized, design remains integral, and costs come down.

With the panel production model in place, Chatman went to work on energy-efficiency. The panels created a high-performance envelope for the house, but his thinking went further, making the houses adaptable while still retaining their environmentally sound qualities. Combining solar energy with methods using biomass and wood, rainwater collection and grey-water recycling, the architect created what he calls a 'pick-and-mix' array of options for energy use/generation. The house can be used with standard connections to public services and energy, or it can operate fully off-grid for use in isolated environments. And there are a range of possibilities in between, using some elements of each in combination.

The designs are adaptable as well. In this dwelling, the two shelters set across the deck take the familiar trope of 'indoor—outdoor living', and almost turn it on its head. In response to traditional building types, Chatman says, he 'deliberately stripped away the vernacular verandah, which typified the local residential building'. Instead, his aim was 'to lightly balance the building on the landscape', a feeling that comes through as it is viewed across the horizon. That experience is only bettered by being welcomed inside, or onto the deck with the whole outdoors to wonder at.

4

BIG IDEAS
FOR LOW
ENERGY

Now that the green imperative has become more pervasive, at least in the realm of newly built houses, we can expect that most buildings will contain some element of an energy-conscious strategy. But really efficient new housing is still far from the global norm, even in Western countries, where the technologies and materials are readily available. That a much better level of energy use and conservation can be achieved is made glaringly obvious by the projects in this chapter. Even though some of them (such as those in the Solar Decathlon section) are the result of work by large teams from architecture and engineering backgrounds working to a competitive brief, their accomplishments are still very real and should be possible to replicate in the more general public realm, with the right will.

For the projects here are not weighed down by their energy-efficient remit, but uplifted by the challenge. As in the best micro-buildings, where the decision to build small sparks innovations in materials, form and light, the commitment to the principle of energy-conservation prompts a more creative approach to every aspect of a structure. This is because each function needs to be thought through carefully in order to make a credible difference in energy-saving and, in many cases, affordability. Of course, there is also the motivation of just trying to do things better – once you begin to build in a new way, the impetus to improve on the old models is hard to stop.

At least, that seems to be the case in every one of the projects that follows. Norwegian architect Sami Rintala is trying to inspire people, especially those living in colder climates, to consider their spatial needs with regard to heating large houses in winter. His Boxhome (p. 142) is an attempt to address the culture of excess in Western society and to create 'a peaceful small home, an urban cave'. Schemata's Paco 3M3 (p. 138) is a similar exercise in reduction; fitting all of the necessary functions into a white cube of 3 cubic metres (106 cubic feet) is a statement that is both artful and an exercise in ingenuity. Both houses take energy use as a primary concern.

The remainder of the chapter is devoted to projects that were part of the Solar Decathlon competition in 2009 and the first European event in 2010. The designs created by university teams for this competition have become sophisticated, high-quality examples of habitation. They not only function well on a small scale, but they include truly innovative solutions to energy creation and conservation. Cornell University's Silo House (p. 147) and Ohio State University's Solar House I (p. 152) both represent attempts to bring an array of energy-efficient strategies to bear in dwellings that also refer to local native architecture.

From Solar Decathlon 2010, which was held in Madrid, we've included five examples, as each brings a new and exciting development to the search for more sustainable and better-quality housing. Innovative designs combine with groundbreaking technologies in entries from the US, Germany, France and Spain. These 'solar' houses demonstrate that much greener housing is both achievable and can offer a more comfortable, even luxurious, lifestyle, and these can be made affordable to the larger population.

LIFTING THE LID

PACO 3M3
Jo Nagasaka and Schemata Architecture Office
Tokyo, Japan
3m³ (106 ft³)

This is a project that ticks a lot of boxes with regard to small buildings: it's micro, it's portable, it's buildable and it reduces energy use by reducing space, which shrinks demand. The white cube has been done before, many times, but not in a model that is quite so bursting with solutions as this. Jo Nagasaka and the Schemata Architecture Office have created a little box of surprises, not only in the fact that it holds so many features cleverly hidden in its floor and attachable to its interior, but also in that it is designed to be partly customized to order. Here, the white cube becomes almost a blank slate, a starting point, like the best in small designs, to allow creativity, enhancement and the personalized details that make a home.

With its pure-white interior, the Paco 3M3 house doesn't at first appear as welcoming as it soon becomes. But then the roof raises a little to let in more light and air. The glazed roof window tilts to an angle, redefining the shape of the interior. The only furniture is a free-standing sink unit, but then a compartment in the floor reveals a little pop-up table. Another underfloor space holds a shower area; the curtain, also white, hanging like an inverted umbrella, is then stowed by its curved handle on a handy wall hook. A further floor compartment contains the toilet. A hammock can be suspended from the roof, which, when the lid is open, allows for a relaxed perch with a view to the outdoors. A further sleeping cubby is tucked into the base of the unit, accessed from a low door outside. It's all pretty cosy, but ultimately functional. Paco 3M3 presents the well-planned interior like a gift, ready to be unpacked.

'I wanted to make something that was between architecture and a product, something people might buy on impulse.'

Schemata is a relatively young practice, but one with a fair number of projects to its credit, including numerous interiors. In a range of schemes, from cafés to galleries, private apartments to church interiors, they demonstrate a feel for materials, not just a stripping away to the minimum. Yet while there is a classic minimalist aspect, as evident in the Paco model, there is also a feel for and appreciation of materials: concrete, rough and polished; wood, natural and stained; and the transformative quality of glass.

The Paco 3M3 is designed to be independent, totally transportable. It is, the architects say, 'about imagining a whole new lifestyle'. And while the vision might be a bit extreme for many people, the project gives new meaning to the term 'pared down', at least in architectural terms. The architects see it being used in a variety of settings, as they describe them: 'house+Paco', 'factory+Paco', 'sea+Paco'. So the concept is to take the house with you, but also to have few requirements for energy and services once you get to your required destination. The idea has great potential, both in terms of reducing the footprint of single dwellings and for influencing an awareness of not just of living beyond our means, but beyond our needs.

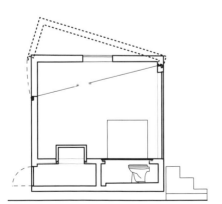

The Paco 3M3 unit is an expandable cube. The roof lifts to let in light and add dimension to the space. Toilet, shower and desk/table are located in the floor, and accessed through removable panels. A sleeping area is also tucked under the floor space.

IN THE BOX

BOXHOME
Rintala Eggertsson Architects
Oslo, Norway
19m² (205 sq ft)

Finnish architect Sami Rintala is passionate about conscientious, sustainable building. He made a name for himself in 1999 with his 'Land(e)scape' project, which involved putting three abandoned barns on 10m- (33 ft-) high legs and moving them into the city, drawing attention to the loss of small, independent farms. He then created the 'Sixty-Minute Man' for the 2000 Venice Biennale, a ship filled with a garden planted on sixty minutes' worth of human waste. As a teacher, Rintala is involved with TYIN Tegnestue (p. 198), a group whose aim is to carry out design-build schemes to produce very basic shelter or services in areas of conflict, natural disaster or poverty across the globe.

As part of the architecture firm of Rintala Eggertsson, Rintala continues to produce structures that are refined and efficient, striking a note of elemental grace with purity of materials and simplicity of form. In his view, a small house makes sense. It should satisfy basic needs, and demand only the minimum of resources. So he created the Boxhome, a pure, rectilinear volume that provides the space for basic functions set within beautifully warm, wood-lined interiors. With this project, Rintala wanted to counter the growing demand for larger and larger houses, all of which, in Scandinavia at least, must be heated for more than half the year, and to challenge the idea that growing prosperity means a further demand for second homes. Rintala proposes a step back to a more energy-conscious, less extravagant lifestyle, one in which the resources themselves are a form of luxury.

The Boxhome, he says, 'focuses on the quality of space, material and natural light, and tries to reduce unnecessary floor area'. As a result, the dwelling costs only about a quarter of what a similarly sized flat would in the Oslo town centre. Even though this structure represents the bare minimum in space, it is not meant to be prescriptive. Rintala produced the Boxhome as a prototype, with the idea that modules could be enlarged or added to create rooms for a family, or to serve as a model for a workplace.

As the architect argues, making a simple house is not a difficult task, nor one that needs to be left to developers and market forces. But though it bespeaks a very satisfying simplicity, the Boxhome is more sophisticated than a simple shelter. It has a balloon frame in standard pine, but other materials are thoughtfully chosen: cypress for the interior walls and floors, birch for the kitchen, spruce in the bathroom, red oak in the living room and nutwood for the bedroom. Aluminium panels on the façade shift around horizontal and vertical window panels, breaking up the cubic appearance into something more dynamic and filling the interior with changing light and shadow. Services are kept on the ground floor, up a vertical ladder is a living-room platform, and slightly above it is a sleeping platform with a skylight that brings light down to the lower rooms.

Rintala maintains that in Western societies we are currently enjoying the highest standard of living ever known to humankind, while also being fully aware of the consequences of consumerism. So it is easy to understand our impact on the environment and to minimize it, and it is an obligation. But with the Boxhome, that duty seems somehow less onerous and more beautiful than it sounds.

'The goal has been to make a peaceful small home, a kind of urban cave, to which a person can withdraw and, whenever wished, forget the intensity of the surrounding city for awhile.'

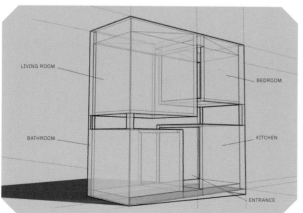

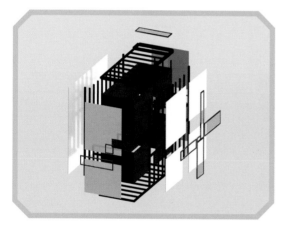

LIVING ROOM

BEDROOM

BATHROOM

KITCHEN

ENTRANCE

The aluminium is a kind of 'city jacket', says Rintala, while the interior is more universal.

Wood used in the four rooms of the house includes 'thermo-treated' birch in the kitchen, oak for the shelves and platforms in the living room, and spruce, traditionally used in Finnish saunas, for the bathroom. The house was transported in two container-sized pieces and then assembled on site.

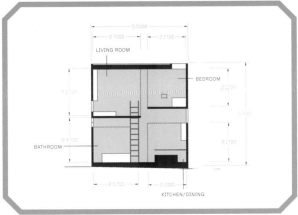

LIVING ROOM

BEDROOM

BATHROOM

KITCHEN/DINING

SOLAR DECATHLON COMPETITION

When looking for great models of small houses, one has to leave a lot of space for the projects that have emerged from the Solar Decathlon competition. Begun in 2002 and sponsored by the US Department of Energy, its stated aim is to 'challenge twenty collegiate teams to design, build and operate solar-powered houses that are cost-effective, energy-efficient and attractive. The winner of the competition is the team that best blends affordability, consumer appeal and design excellence with optimal energy production and maximum efficiency.' The 'decathlon' label refers to ten separate categories by which each project is judged, such as 'architecture', 'innovation', 'sustainability' and 'engineering'. During the final weeks of the competition, the structures are rebuilt on the National Mall in Washington, DC, where the public can visit and judges can compare entries on one site.

In 2010 Madrid hosted the first-ever Solar Decathlon Europe, with the entries erected under the direct sun, where temperatures reached more than 40º C (104º F). Inside, the houses remained cool and comfortable, all the while generating nearly three times the energy they consumed over the ten-day competition. Over the years, Solar Decathlon has become a serious, and increasingly international, competition. And with every year the design stakes have grown higher as the forms and internal programmes have become ever-more sophisticated. The entries featured here from the 2009 and 2010 events vary on style and approach, but all of them take a holistic view of energy efficiency, using materials that are low cost and low energy, while also making use of complex, integrated computer systems to monitor usage and energy generation.

SOLAR SPACES

SILO HOUSE
Cornell University
Solar Decathlon 2009, USA
47m² (506 sq ft)

Christopher Werner was the lead designer of the project for Cornell University for Solar Decathlon 2009, and his team produced a building that was perhaps the most iconic, and yet the most unusual, of the competition. By drawing on the materials and forms of the grain silos of the American Midwest, the team came up with a tripartite scheme with each 'silo' housing a separate function. The aim, says Werner, was not just to design a competitive entry, but also to 'prove the potential of creative design in a "green" building'.

The form is comprised of three cylinders, one each for housing areas for sleeping, eating and living. Yet double-functions and efficient use of space are everywhere. The kitchen island contains an energy-efficient induction stove top and open dining area, as well as containing a refrigerator, dishwasher, convection oven and room for storage. A bathroom is tucked in next to the bedroom area, where the bed, on a counter-weighted pulley system, can be drawn up into a concealed ceiling box. The very considered arrangement of amenities allows much more open space than one would have thought possible, aided by the fact that the three 'rooms' are all orientated towards the rectilinear courtyard, which has been covered in decking. A folding window-wall system allows all of the spaces (or none) to be open to each other and to the circulation area of the open deck.

The Corten corrugated steel shell reflects the local industrial–agricultural aesthetic of rural buildings in the northern reaches of Upstate New York, but also aids with energy retention. Solar gain from the steel envelope is captured for use through a 'skin-integrated solar thermal

The two chairs in the living room are made from reclaimed bourbon barrels. Locally sourced, sustainably forested black locust, ash and beech hardwoods were used for the interior, with zero off-gassing materials used for finishes throughout. The plan shows the arrangement of the three circular rooms, set around a covered deck area.

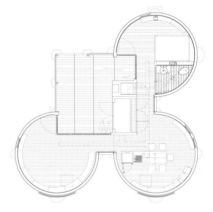

system' that preheats water for the house. In essence, the heat captured by the steel is transferred to water running through copper pipes behind the cladding. The warmed water can then be heated further through the primary heat source: a hot-water tank, in which sixty vacuum-sealed glass tubes heat an antifreeze solution and transfer heat through a heat exchanger. Each cylinder has openable skylights for ventilation, and diffuse natural light beneath the canopy of photovoltaic sheets. Electricity is supplied by sheets that hover above the silos and the porch. The forty panels are angled slightly for rainwater run-off, and can produce 38 kilowatt-hours of energy on a sunny autumn day. To keep track of the consumption and creation of energy,

a 'smart distribution panel' houses an Internet-connected circuit breaker that monitors the house's twenty-four circuits. Software that allows the circuits to be switched on or off as needed further refines consumption.

For many people, even those who are energy-conscious, tracking their own usage and finding ways to be more efficient is still something of a puzzle. With a national grid system, we have all become somewhat disconnected from the energy supply that we tap into daily. Of all the energy-efficient features in this house, perhaps the most effective is the immediate access to information about how much energy we use each day in the tasks and amenities we have come to take so much for granted. But it is perhaps the evolution of

the humble grain silo to such a level of design and sophistication that best signifies the project's far-reaching yet democratic aims.

OHIO IN THE SUN

SOLAR HOUSE I
Ohio State University
Solar Decathlon 2009, USA
50.2m² (538 sq ft)

Perhaps the most remarkable aspect of the successful Solar
Decathlon projects is the amount of collaboration involved in
the conception, design and construction of each entry. For
Ohio State's first foray into the competition, no fewer than
sixty students and faculty participated, so the house is not
only an achievement in creating an energy-saving domestic
space, but also in coordination and communication. The team
decided that the house should have a localized perspective,
and 're-address Midwestern American living'. This was a
significant first step in that it focused the function of the
house to a particular climate, but, perhaps more importantly,
it also challenged certain attitudes in aspiring to houses of
ever-larger footprints and energy consumption.

The first two steps towards more compact living were
to reduce the house's overall footprint and to increase
flexibility within the main space. Solar House I was designed
to be used by two people, and to accommodate entertaining
for eight. It does this by having furnishings that can be
tucked into storage hidden around the perimeter. The
rationale is simple enough, but the execution in this
attractive, high-functioning little house is where the real
achievement lies. The third component in the design is the
layer of energy-saving devices that are built into the walls,
creating both a high-performance thermal layer and a
system of ventilation, shading and energy creation. Doors
pivot with louvres mounted on aluminium frames, so they can
be opened in various configurations to allow in light and
heat. A reflecting pond on the western elevation helps to
cool air that will then draw through low-level vents to
refresh the interior in warm weather. A trombe wall is

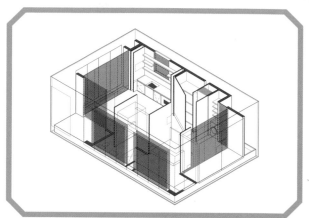

layered with a polycarbonate glazing panel behind a 20cm (8 in) air gap, in which full-height acrylic tubes, filled with water, absorb the sun's energy during the day and release it into the interior. A system of evacuated tubes on the south wall and on the roof heats water for domestic use and for the radiant heating indoors.

The most distinctive feature of the house is its weathered board siding, which was taken from an old barn. The naturally silvered timber gives the house, for all of its technical advances, a solid connection to the local vernacular, suggesting that living smaller and more efficiently isn't quite such a foreign concept, but might just be possible closer to home.

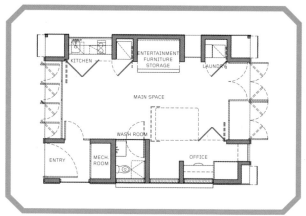

Pivoting doors that open onto the deck also modulate light and heat into the open-plan interior. The external cladding was reclaimed from a local disused barn.

Previous pages: The trombe wall was filled with white polycarbonate glazing over acrylic tubing, which takes in heat during the day and transfers it to the interior at night. Louvres control the solar gain throughout the year.

THE LIGHTS ARE ON

LUMENHAUS

Virginia Tech University
Solar Decathlon Europe 2010, Spain
62m² (667 sq ft)

'The best way to address issues of energy in buildings is to use as little as possible,' say the designers from Virginia Tech, who created the Lumenhaus. The team competed against seventeen international research universities, ultimately winning the 2010 event in Madrid with their boldly ambitious model of energy efficiency by using the most advanced technologies, together with comfortable modern design. Embracing the concept of 'responsive architecture', the house is equipped to generate its own energy and create a comfortable living environment, and to do so while continually adapting to changing weather conditions, making best use of its advanced capabilities. A simple, rectilinear form, with surrounding deck area and two reflecting ponds to expand the living space to the outdoors, the Lumenhaus has all of the attributes of a well-designed modern home. But there is a great deal more to it than meets the eye. High-quality insulation, high-performance units, solar panels and a centrally controlled operations system all contribute to the effective use of energy in a compact domestic environment.

The most arresting feature of this programme for sustainable living is the series of sliding screens that form the outermost layer of the walls. Inspired by the mushrabiyah of traditional Arab houses, the screens are made from stainless steel punched with disk-shaped cut-outs. These comprise the 'Eclipsis' system, a programme of subtle complexity that serves several functions beyond the obvious use of screening sunlight. The rotation of each of the nine thousand disks was determined by sophisticated Grasshopper software, which was developed to calculate the angle of the sun and the degree of visibility in different areas of the house. When the screens are pulled to, these aspects are carefully attenuated. As architect and faculty member Robert Dunay explains, 'there is more rotation of the discs from the floor upward, so it gets lighter as you go up'. The amount of exposure also changes depending on where you are in the house. 'You don't see a clear view standing in the dining area,' Dunay adds, 'but you do at head height when you are seated at the dining table.' In addition, the screens allow for cross-ventilation when closed, while also providing security. Lastly, but perhaps most importantly to the overall ambience of the interior, the closed screens produce a pleasing pattern of natural light and shadow, which is not unlike the feeling of sitting beneath a leafy tree.

Beyond the multifunctioning outer screens, there are further layers of clever design and engineering. Another set of sliding panels, made from polycarbonate filled with Aerogel to provide a layer of effective insulation, seal the house to the elements, while still allowing the passage of muted natural light. Indoors, the concrete floor collects and emits passive heat and is laid over a hydronic system, using radiant hot-water heating tubes. The roof is a combination of tilting solar panels and a white membrane that reflects sunlight to the back side of the panels, providing an efficiency increase of 10 to 30 per cent. The whole system is informed by the 'weather station' mounted outside, a slim pole topped with sensors that relay information on temperature and atmosphere to the house's central computer system, which is controlled by an iPad interface that monitors the energy use throughout the house.

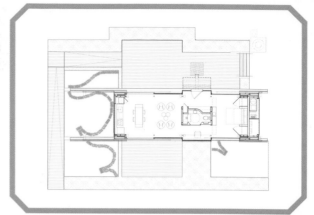

'The weather station is the central point of our concept of "responsive architecture",' says team member Joseph Wheeler. 'As information is relayed from the sensors throughout the building, the screens and insulation panels open or close, optimizing energy use and comfort.' Of course, the system can be overridden, and users can open and close screens manually, altering the light and ventilation as they see fit.

While the idea of counting every change in condition and energy use might point towards some eco-neurosis, the fact that it can all be left to care for itself — because the efficiency is already embedded in the design — is a liberating concept. Enjoyment of the cosy, wood-lined modern interior or a living area expanded to an open deck and unbridled fresh air is made more luxurious in the knowledge that it isn't literally costing the earth.

The design calls for surrounding ponds that help to cool air as it enters the house. Even with the screens closed, the interior still receives plenty of natural light.

The plan shows the kitchen and sleeping areas at either end, with a core at the centre that contains the bathroom. The key to the flexible design is the built-in, retractable furniture, including the sofa/ bed, cupboard and table.

WELL HINGED

IKAROS HOUSE
University of Applied Sciences Rosenheim
Solar Decathlon Europe 2010, Spain
60m² (646 sq ft)

Though the Lumenhaus project (p. 156) took the overall prize at Solar Decathlon Europe 2010, it beat the next-place competition, Ikaros House, by only one point. But the minute scoring is more a tribute to the level of competition than a product of close accounting. Ikaros employs a similarly effective system of movable steel screens, but here the screens are formed of hundreds of hinged 'zig-zag' plates that open or collapse as the screens are raised or lowered over the large windows. Set up on generous wood decking, the house presents itself as a textured, rectangular volume, with corners cut out at either end of a diagonal, creating a covered entry at the front and a private lounging area at the back. The interior is cool and chic, full of the most advanced energy-saving devices and top-of-the-line appliances.

Multifunctionality is a requisite of the best designs. Here, a tall cupboard rolls out into the living space to make room for a bed behind it, the kitchen counter slides open to reveal the stove top, and a flat-screen TV dips into a pocket to make more room for an extendable dining table. The slim-profile construction makes use of a smaller volume of materials, and was made possible through a special wood-steel adhesive joint, which gives surface gain to the interior space, and the use of vacuum insulation panels. Because of the highly insulated construction, heating costs were substantially lower than in a conventional building, even in Rosenheim's markedly cooler climate. Behind the collapsing zig-zag screens, oversized windows afford the minimal interior a much more expansive feeling. But because of the optimized building envelope and thermally efficient triple-glazing, that effect does not result in inefficient heat

Hinged steel plates make up the screens, which can be raised to shade the windows or lowered for greater solar gain. For cooling, rainwater collected in a cistern is sprayed over the roof at night.

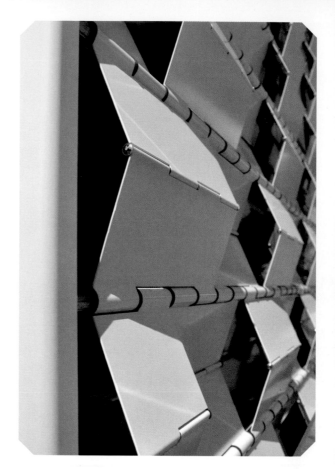

loss. With the screens open, the passive gain is effective in providing heat even from the winter sun.

Cooling the house in high temperatures was accomplished by a two-pronged approach. Firstly, a phase-changing material (PCM) – which changes from liquid to solid and back again, according to the temperature – was used as a latent heat accumulator, absorbing and storing heat through its transition. Then, water circulated within the roof system in the evening air was used as part of a cooling system for the house during the day. In addition to these passive measures, a compression heat pump can be used when necessary (with electricity for this and all of the house supplied by the rooftop solar panels). Despite, and because of, these technical innovations, the house has a very contemporary appeal. The minimally sized interior has great flexibility with the collapsing bedroom area, and even additional pull-out beds for guests. These touches provide the impromptu air of student accommodation, while the sophisticated workings of the house, its elegant design and energy-economy all point to a much more grown-up attitude to long-term living and the environment.

According to its enthusiastic team of designers and engineers, the Ikaros House generates four times as much energy as it uses, and its efficient heating and cooling envelope saves 14,000kg (30,865 lbs) on CO_2 emissions over a standard house per year. That's about the same quantity of emissions created by driving 160,934 km (100,000 miles) in the average (European) car. But it's a tribute to this innovative, thoughtful design that sitting in the house felt like a celebration, even before the awards were handed out.

The design is composed of four modules: the entrance, bedroom and work room; the walkway; the kitchen and bathroom; and the living room with terrace. A mobile storage unit (seen left) can be pulled further into the living space to open up the bedroom area on the other side.

The layers of wall structure allow migration of water vapour towards the exterior to reduce damp indoors. Materials 'breathe', so there is no need for a vapour barrier, and reduced need for extra ventilation.

The wood used for the house was taken from forests near the school in Bordeaux. The cladding was created from a special process in which the knots are taken out of the sheets and the ends are pressed together to make longer, sturdier single pieces. All paint is ecologically safe. West and north-facing sides are dark, south- and east-facing are of lighter wood.

FABULOUS

FABLAB HOUSE
IAAC with the MIT Center for Bits and Atoms
Solar Decathlon Europe 2010, Spain
59m^2 (635 sq ft) + deck

It looks as if it could have fallen from a giant tree, or crawled up from a tropical sphere, but too much musing on form misses the point. It is, according to the team of students and faculty who created it, 'a paraboloid section positioned for suitable solar tracking and deformed in appropriate steps aimed towards an optimal orientation for summer (narrowing to the west, widening eastward, and flattening towards the zenith of 70°)'. In summary, the point of the FabLab House is to get as much solar energy and provide as much living space as possible within a compact, thermally efficient, low-cost structure. It's part of a 'form follows energy' approach, in which, the team argue, 'the house is no longer a machine, but an organism to be inhabited'.

'FabLab' stands for 'fabrication laboratories', and the branch responsible for the project, based at the IAAC in Barcelona, is one of several set up by MIT's Center for Bits and Atoms at locations around the world. Using the latest-generation digital machines, the team create prototypes and scale models for architecture, construction and industrial design. They specialize in projects that require a direct connection from design (via computer) to machinery for processing materials according to digital instructions. In this spirit, the FabLab House was prefabricated from wooden parts that were all digitally specified and cut using CNC technology. All of the structural components were taken from a single sheet of laminated veneer lumber, and were then assembled into twenty parts and transported to the site, where they were lifted into place.

That such a highly technical, computer-driven process would produce such an organic-looking structure highlights the shift in the past few decades from the production of the uniformly modular towards the individually customized. In this case, customization is working towards the maximum energy gain and efficiency of use. Keeping in mind its solar relationship and the fact of its being a carbon sink, wood was chosen as the main building material. And, the team point out, the use of wood, in comparison with steel or concrete, 'leads to structural elements and components that are small, lightweight and manageable'. The timber-frame structure was covered by a shell created from small sections of 5mm (2 in) ply, which give the building its armoured appearance. The panels are very flexible when bent with the grain, so that they can be placed on a curve without cracking. These were then coated with varnish to protect against rain. The solar panels, which cover a section of the upper (roof) structure, are actually thin 'sheets', and were specially developed for the project. They are thin and bendy, and the curved surface helps to absorb sunlight as it changes angle and position.

As the project was designed to suit the hot, summer temperatures of Madrid, the team took care to provide shaded outdoor space and solve the problem of plant storage at the same time. Three legs raise the building off the ground, creating a large, shaded area for lounging or outdoor dining. Hidden within the legs are services, equipment and water (incoming and outgoing). With its technical pedigree and biotic shape, the FabLab House seems to embody the concept of a 'living house'; that is, a structure that is both highly advanced and somehow reassuringly of the earth.

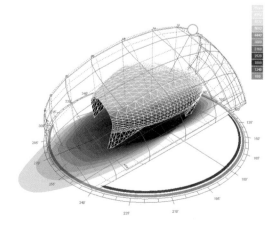

The house is built exclusively of timber, with all components cut from laminated veneered lumber using CNC technology. The three legs contain the services. An internal control system provides detailed 'real-time' monitoring of the house's performance.

'The mobile elements are very important – the bar, the herb garden and trees, and the pull-out sofas – all of which allow inhabitants to use the space in different ways.'

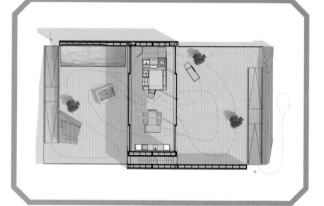

The signature element of the house is the 'smartbox', an internal unit that contains the bathroom/storage on the ground floor, and an elevated sleeping alcove, with a window overlooking the living space. The entire kitchen counter unit with built-in coffee machine and shelves can be rolled out onto the rear deck and used for al-fresco dining.

5

BIG IDEAS
MULTIPLIED

In this chapter, we look at designs that are conceived for replication, a process that lends itself particularly to the compact and prefabricated. The projects that follow are of seeming extremes: the holiday cottage, symbolizing luxury and leisure; and social housing, offering basic shelter and services. Presenting these two ends of the spectrum is not so much about contrast, but commonality. Just as looking at small buildings was never meant to be an exclusive exercise, but one meant to inform what could be achieved at different scales for different purposes, so examining one well-executed small house can help further the aims of another.

Holiday houses have an intrinsic appeal that a domestic dwelling, however well built, cannot approach. But through their innovative construction methods and ingenious concepts, the schemes here go well beyond the offer of pleasant holiday accommodation. Located in the Pennsylvania woods near Frank Lloyd Wright's masterful Fallingwater, a small array of cottages by Patkau Architects (p. 194) sets one example for using the land well and taking one's cue from nature. Much farther afield, on the protected and remote Easter Island, Chilean firm AATA have produced a small cluster of wonderfully inviting wood cabins (p. 186) that combine climatic concerns with inspired forms and materials. And in the Swedish countryside, the provocative approach of VisionDivision to the traditional holiday compound (p. 204) reminds us that sometimes you have to push the boat out to see what's possible on the horizon.

Offering a link between luxury and necessity is Joseph Bellomo, who created a quick-build structure that can be used to create a backyard studio or emergency shelter (p. 190). His House Arc prototype reminds us of the ways in which disaster-relief shelters are an enduring conundrum. How temporary or mobile should they be? What materials can be gathered most cheaply and effectively? The work of Norwegian collective TYIN Tegnestue is among those few designs that have actually made their way into the most desperate areas. Their sleeping huts for Karen orphans on the Thai-Burmese border (p. 198), while not complete houses, go a long way towards creating something like a home. Addressing the issues of good design together with site and community is the aim of the Chilean firm Elemental, who have made a name for themselves with ambitious and humane schemes for public housing (p. 208). Elemental are facing the challenge of housing the urban poor, whose numbers are set to increase rapidly in the next twenty years. While taking on housing in the urban environment is a challenge in itself, Polish architect Ryszard Rychlicki has chosen one of the least salubrious of settings – the pockets around motorways – to create a model for housing students and other transient populations by redesigning the way houses and the people in them can breathe (p. 182).

The concept presented at the beginning of the book – considering how much space we really need before we start to design up – is one way of using what can be learned here. So holiday and disaster shelter, mobile and permanent structures, solar-powered and grid-dependent buildings, all keep us moving from small structures to a larger impact – ever-better and more conscientious design.

BREATHING SPACE

INSTANT LUNG
Ryszard Rychlicki, 2RAM
Milan, Italy
32m² (344 sq ft)

An image of people wearing wartime-style gas masks doesn't immediately excite enthusiasm for a design project. But young architect Ryszard Rychlicki uses the illustrations to capture a theme that propels this project from being just another reslicing of the minimal box. Focusing on both the urban living space and the living space poisoned by pollution, Rychlicki has made a determined stab at improving the city-dweller's quality of life. And he does it by taking on the most primal element of life: air. This is not a scheme about rooftop gardens or low-density building, but about architecture that is able, quite literally, to improve the air we breathe.

The idea was to come up with a scheme for a housing development that could exist in the hinterland around the urban motorway, while making the units more habitable, perhaps pleasantly so, and far less toxic than a standard house set down in such an unwelcoming environment. To accomplish this, the architect concentrated on the problems of eliminating exhaust fumes and noise. Further to this challenge was the attempt to create multiple, affordable small housing units, and to make them easy and quick to build, in keeping with the theme of the Instant House exhibition in Milan, for which the design was developed in 2009. The key feature of Rychlicki's house is the eponymous, accordion-like central 'lung', which takes in air through a narrow, vertical gap in the external wall and filters it through to the interior rooms. The lung is made of sixty-nine elements of glue-laminated timber, combined with wooden blocks that create the framework for air circulation. This structure is then covered with a 'breathing' material of cotton and felt, which will trap unwanted pollutants inside,

while allowing cleaner air through. Rising and twisting through the two-level volume, the lung is exposed to all the rooms in the house; indeed, its structure helps to create the stair and upstairs sleeping area.

Noise pollution is another target of Rychlicki's design. This is a challenge that in many city projects is left to be answered by glazing alone. The Instant Lung does include special U-glass with high soundproofing qualities, but there is also soundproofing embedded in the structural walls. The exterior is something of a compromise in affordability and function. Because of the corroding effects of pollution, the architect chose to use precast, reinforced concrete for the structure and external cladding, with the idea that the outside character will somehow be 'integrated with the sceneries of the motorway'. With the filter working so hard to better the environment for residents, one hopes that the exterior of the house can work a bit harder towards doing the same.

Rychlicki sums up his thinking by saying that he 'transferred the air-filtering mask and the soundproof headphones to the function of a house', and 'decided to put the filter into a simple, soundproof form'. It certainly sounds simple enough. And most new housing schemes now give some thought to adequate and efficient ventilation, if not to active air purification. Perhaps it is the overt physicality of the method that is so striking (if not alarming) in this scheme. With the 'lung' renderings set alongside those masks, the project threatens to veer towards science fiction, and the associations seem deliberate. Like those graphic warnings on cigarette labels, the Instant Lung calls attention to danger that we ignore at our peril.

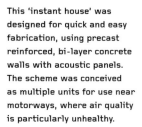

This 'instant house' was designed for quick and easy fabrication, using precast reinforced, bi-layer concrete walls with acoustic panels. The scheme was conceived as multiple units for use near motorways, where air quality is particularly unhealthy.

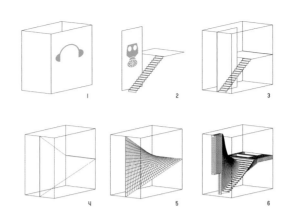

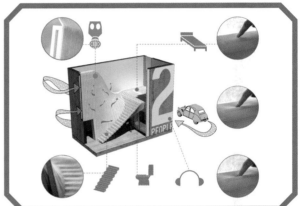

The house is divided into zones by the central filter, or 'lung', a twisted plane that becomes furniture – stairs, beds, chairs, shelves – and is entirely covered in felt and cotton. The house can be expanded to 40m² (431 sq ft) to accommodate four people.

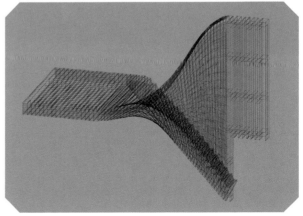

LESSONS OF THE PAST

MORERAVA COTTAGES
AATA Arquitectos
Easter Island, Chile
60m² (646 sq ft)

It is the most isolated habitable land in the world, 2,250 km (1,400 miles) from the nearest inhabited island and about 3,475 km (2,000 miles) from the nearest population centres of Chile and Tahiti. It is about 166 km² (64 sq miles) in area. The natives call the island Te Pito te-henua, meaning 'land's end', although it is more commonly known by the official Chilean names Isla de Pascua and Rapa Nui. Listed as a UNESCO World Heritage site, the island is volcanic and has a fragile eco-system. There are no rivers, and the only fresh water is in the three volcanic crater lakes. It is thought that the original inhabitants contributed to their own demise by overhunting several species of land birds for food, and by cutting down the native palms to use as rollers to move the gigantic moai statues that ring the perimeter of the island. Even now the island has very few trees.

With a native population of fewer than four thousand, Easter Island has a variety of tourist accommodation available, mainly through guest houses, not all of which are particularly eco-conscious. These new cabins, however, designed by Chilean firm AATA Arquitectos, take their ecological remit very seriously. Though there is, rather surprisingly, no regulation of what can be built on the island, the architects decided to restrict themselves to buildings that had as little impact on the environment as possible. The wood-framed and wood-clad buildings are comparatively lightweight, requiring less intrusive foundations, but designed to cope with the occasional high winds and heavy rains of the island. Rainwater is collected on the roof of each structure, and then treated and stored for use. In this way, architect Sebastián Cerda Pé explains, the cottages 'avoid the overconsumption of a resource that is already rare on the island'. Solar panels provide all of the cottages' electricity, while water is heated by way of a solar-heating system. These methods alleviate the need for external power, which on the island is provided by petrol.

In addition to their green aspect, the cottages have been finished in a design that combines the native Polynesian open-air style with clean, modern spaces. The basic rectilinear plan makes an efficient use of the spaces, which run from front to back, with the volume open at each end to a deck area, an amenity that is both appealing and very practical in such a temperate climate. The trapezoidal forms appear to be wrapped in their smooth, timber cladding. The material folds up from floor to wall to roof, leaving a line of clerestory windows along one elevation and ground-level openings on the opposite wall. These are part of a strategy of cross-ventilation, which is key during the warmer months. Windows and openings also take best advantage of natural sunlight and reduce the need for electric lighting.

On first inspection, it isn't the environmentally friendly or efficient design that is most striking, but the beauty of the pure natural wood and the elegance of the structures, both singularly and as a rhythmic array. These aspects raise the cottages to a level of design that complements the natural setting, which is so unique even among its island neighbours. If the island's past is a warning on a micro-level of man's ability to cause his own destruction through overexploitation of resources, then the Morerava Cottages are a definite sign of hope that lessons are being learned.

Materials for the cottages came from Chile; as the architects point out, 'the idea was not to use the island's resources'. The design responds to local weather conditions, giving special attention to cross-ventilation and lightweight construction, without the need for high thermal performance.

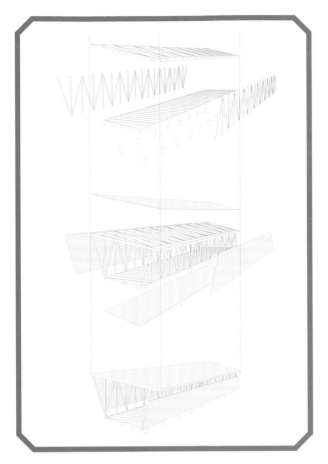

The exploded diagram
shows the simple assembly
programme. Along one side,
the wall is solid from the roof
nearly to the floor, allowing
low-level ventilation. Along
the other, the windows form
a clerestory, ensuring that air
moves throughout the space.

TUBULAR THINKING

HOUSE ARC
Joseph Bellomo Architects
Hawaii, USA
70m² (753 sq ft)

It all started with bicycles. Several years ago, the green-minded, California-based architect Joseph Bellomo teamed up with cycling enthusiast Jeff Selzer to create a lightweight, easily installed, compact bicycle-storage unit that could be deployed in parking lots, around parks and in city centres. The resulting Bike Arc was a curved structure made of tubular steel ribs and covered with semi-opaque polycarbonate. The design was later cleverly modified for different climates and environments. Sticking to the basic idea of a curved-rib structure covered in weatherproof material, Bellomo and his design leader, Taraneh Naddafi, transferred the model to the problem of housing, and came up with the House Arc: a prefabricated design that could be used in single units (and deployed as emergency shelter), or combined to form a multi-unit dwelling. The first unit, not a complete house but a single-room addition for an existing building, was erected on the island of Hawaii in 2010.

True to Bellomo's green reputation, the House Arc is designed to function off-grid, and would be 'ideally fabricated locally' wherever it was set up. So its design is remarkably flexible. Rather than being a 'typical modular house with prefabricated panels', Bellomo explains, 'the House Arc is constructed with a kit of parts – individual pieces such as steel ribs, polycarbonate wall panels and cedar wood'. But the choice of cladding material can vary, 'depending on local resources and climate'. The curvilinear frame was carried over from the Bike Arc, not just to adhere to branding, but because the curved structure allows for the addition of such amenities as beds, desks or countertops, while keeping the physical footprint smaller and lighter.

'The House Arc comes with an easy-to-follow, graphic installation manual that requires no special training.'

The built house also works towards energy efficiency. Ventilation and cooling are promoted by way of air flow beneath the raised trellis that hovers above the roof, and under the floor, which sits on concrete piers that are set into the grade or dowelled into the bedrock. Bellomo is currently working with a supplier to provide polycarbonate that is embedded with solar film, a new material that can both function as translucent cladding and generate power at all times of day and in conditions of variable sunshine.

Bellomo likens the construction method to that of flat-pack furniture, meaning it can be cheaply and easily transported and put together on site. The kit-of-parts approach also means a very quick assembly time, which further reduces energy costs. A basic house could be installed by three or four people in as many days. Keeping the structure raised off the ground reduces the permanent impact and allows it to be taken down more easily and transported to another site when necessary.

Though the first built model was not a fully functioning house, 'the future goal of the House Arc', Bellomo says, is to 'rehouse people after catastrophic events and replace housing that was not built to withstand such forces'. It is all a bit more sophisticated than flat-pack furniture or bicycle racks, but by attempting to bring the materials and methods of building to the unskilled user, it goes a long way towards making the distribution of high-quality shelter more humane.

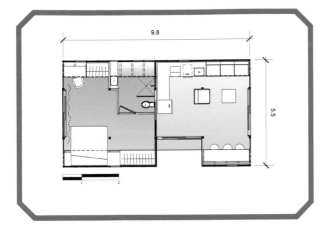

The main ribs are a modular structure of steel tubes. The cladding materials can vary, depending on the local resources and climate. Examples include local woods such as cedar siding, recycled metal panels over a waterproof membrane, and a plywood substrate.

The House Arc can be composed of two modules, one with kitchen and living services, the other with sleeping quarters. These can be joined by a deck to form a breezeway between them.

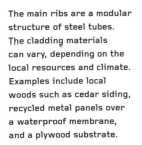

THE NATURE IMPERATIVE

MEADOW COTTAGES
Patkau Architects
Mill Run, Pennsylvania, USA
From 63m² (678 sq ft)

Frank Lloyd Wright's Fallingwater, designed in 1935 for department store magnate Edgar J. Kaufmann, stands as one of the greatest works of American architecture in the 20th century. The audacious feat of setting a house on a rocky cliff, straddling a natural waterfall, would be daunting even for contemporary architects and engineers. But the grace and ingenuity with which Wright executed the design are perhaps unparalleled. So when the Western Pennsylvania Conservancy, the owner of Fallingwater, called for entries for a competition to build half a dozen cottages in the meadowland above the iconic house, it was also throwing down a challenge of some magnitude.

The team who won the chance to take on that challenge was the Canadian firm, Patkau Architects. The key, and possibly the determining, feature of their proposal was the decision to follow Wright's lead in letting the natural terrain dictate, quite literally, the cottages' atmosphere and overall form. 'Just as Fallingwater is an intensification of the rock outcroppings that characterize Bear Run,' architect John Patkau explains, 'the Meadow Cottages are an intensification of the swelling ground plane of the meadow, made from the very soil and grasses of the meadow itself.' So as Wright chose to build from the rock over the falls (rather than siting the house more conventionally below or across from them), Patkau chose to site the new cottages within the undulations of the meadow, instead of on top of them.

The effect, best appreciated when looking directly onto the structures, is of a series of modern, well-lit burrows, tucked securely into the small eruptions of the grassy plain. Inside, the cottages maintain their snug, cave-like effect,

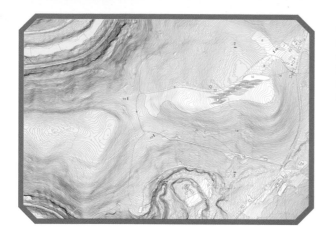

with the interiors formed of curved pockets of space, lit by large frontal openings, tucked-away windows and clerestories. A continuous, smooth wood lining adds to the feeling of a being inside a scooped-out section of earth.

The scheme is much more efficient and adaptable than its unusual design would suggest. The basic building structure and envelope is a standard-sized, corrugated-steel culvert, of a type that is regionally manufactured for industrial and agricultural use. (The more usual sighting of these structures is where they are used for water drainage, beneath roads, and/or in gullies or ditches.) The culvert is wrapped in sheet metal and a waterproof membrane, and insulated on the inside with VOC-free polyurethane foam. The units can be constructed using a choice of methods. They can be assembled on site, as with a conventional detached house, or prefabricated in a factory and shipped to the site, where they are then attached to a cast-in-place concrete foundation slab and then covered with earth. The latter method, obviously, saves energy, labour and waste. Both the

exterior and interior are designed 'for durability and longevity', says Patkau. 'The grasses of the site are a naturally renewable exterior cladding material, the weathering steel ages to a permanent natural finish, and the wood and concrete create a warm, low-maintenance interior.'

For all of the functional, industrial elements, the cottages have distinctively modern, somewhat glamorous interiors, at least from what is promised in the renderings. The internal walls are lined with oak-veneered plywood, which seems to wrap the inhabitants in gold-tinged warmth. With natural light seeping in from the pockets beyond the main portal, the experience of the internal space is also surprisingly varied. Such holistically designed, well-lit and intimate spaces, looking onto and into the surrounding grassland, are something even the exacting master of Fallingwater could appreciate.

Interiors are lined in
oak-veneered ply over a
polyurethane insulation layer.

TAKING FLIGHT

SOE KER TIE HOUSES

TYIN Tegnestue
Noh Bo, Tak, Thailand
6m² (65 sq ft)

There is no doubt that designing for extreme circumstances or times of emergency is a noble endeavour. High-flying notions of beauty, perfection, even efficiency, must be sidelined for the sake of necessity, urgency and humanity. While a number of architects have in recent years come up with some wonderfully innovative designs to address these desperate situations, few of these designs have made it to their actual target in realized form.

TYIN Tegnestue is a non-profit humanitarian group of architecture students based in Trondheim, Norway. In 2008 they became involved with a project to help with the influx of refugees from Burma to emergency settlements on the Thai–Burmese border. A fellow Norwegian, Ole Jørgen Edna, had set up an orphanage in a small village in the Tak province to help with the rising numbers of mainly ethnic Karen people fleeing the conflict. Having taken on twenty-four orphans two years earlier, Edna was now struggling to make room for around fifty. The orphanage needed more and better shelter, but the team thought well beyond the basic physical requirements of architecture. They wanted to 'somehow recreate what these children would have experienced in a more normal situation', and to ensure that each child had their 'own private space, a home to live in, and a neighbourhood where they could interact and play'.

The solution was to create a group of dormitory buildings, which could offer sleeping accommodation that was sturdy, weatherproof and safe, and was also built and arrayed in a way that suggested a life of normality and community. Six simple-seeming diminutive 'houses' are arranged to encourage activities around and through

The houses were set on concrete legs, cast into old car tyres. Two houses are joined by an open breezeway. The houses were placed at different angles and distances to encourage group interaction and form varying spaces for outdoor activities.

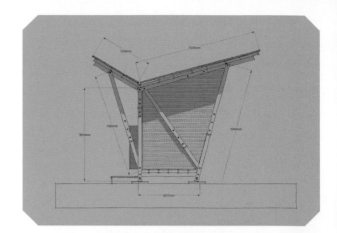

the spaces. The units do not have running water or cooking facilities, but still manage to suggest 'life', rather than bare-bones 'shelter'. Packed into the 450cm- (177 in-) height structures are two levels of sleeping lofts, as well as floor space at ground level for sitting, 'doing homework' or just messing about.

The methodology was simple and effective, but at the same time wonderfully ingenious. Steeply angled roofs increase ventilation and allow for the collection of rainwater. Framing was done in ironwood, with sections prefabricated and assembled on site. To prevent problems with moisture and damp, the houses were raised off the ground, and sat on concrete foundations. A virtue was made of the most plentiful local material – bamboo appears in slender poles that form front wall panels, as strips woven in the traditional style for side and back panels, and in chunky segments set into screens. In addition to these very practical elements, this mini-neighbourhood, with its tidy paths, coloured window shutters and canted roofs, presents a rather joyful oasis in the shadow of so much that is tragic.

The obtuse V-shape inspired the workmen to dub the structures 'Soe Ker Tie', or 'butterfly', houses, but the name denotes more than a similarity of form. The team's aims are forward-looking, as expressed in their mission statement: 'By introducing basic but crucial principles like bracing, moisture prevention and material economization, our projects work as examples to be used by locals in the future.' They also bring in local people to participate in the designing and building process. These are all noble ideas that have, in this instance at least, actually taken wing.

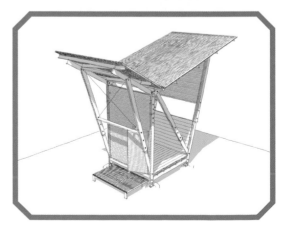

The design features a ground-floor space with two overlapping tiers of sleeping lofts above. When the number of residents grows, the floor space is also used for sleeping. Varied window openings and painted plywood shutters give the houses a playful appeal. Simple outdoor furnishings include a bamboo swing and a chessboard made from a segment of broken water tank.

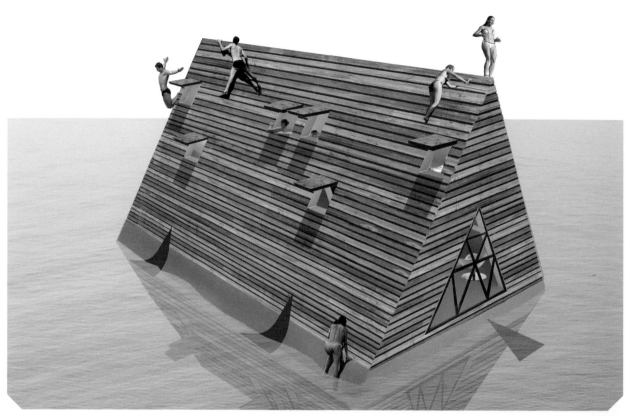

The design as currently produced in Sweden uses the whole trunk of the tree: heart wood on the façade, where its solidity helps to form a protective skin; and outer parts for the interior, where the material is not exposed to weathering.

The A-frame design takes advantage of the stability of the triangular structure and a stacked programme that makes use of the angled roofline. Guest rooms can be accessed via outdoor hatches, which also allow high-level views of the countryside.

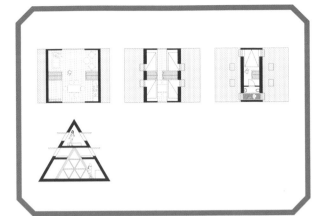

HALFWAY THERE

HALF-A-HOUSE
Elemental Chile
Monterrey, Mexico / Milan, Italy
From 18.6m² (194 sq ft)

Flats, technically, deviate from the topic of small houses, but what Chilean firm Elemental have produced in this arena redefines what is a house and what is a flat. More importantly, their work marks a crucial move towards better and more achievable public housing, questioning the inherent differences in quality between private and public design. Elemental is a 'do-tank' that has put social housing squarely at the forefront of the architecture debate. With an imperative to house a growing population of urban poor, they espouse three fundamental aims: 'to think, design and build better neighbourhoods, housing and infrastructure'; to 'build under the same market and policy conditions as any other [project]'; and to create 'design that guarantees incremental value and returns on investment over time'.

Director Alejandro Aravena has created larger, more commercial projects (including the Siamese Towers at the Universidad Católica de Santiago), but it is his approach in building over a thousand houses for the poor that has won him world-renown as a progenitor of humanitarian design. To challenge the primary ills of social housing (poor-quality design, overcrowding and ghettoized locations), Aravena came up with the 'half-a-house' concept. When the Chilean government presented him with the challenge of housing one hundred families in Iquique, in northern Chile, with only $7,500 for each family, the company faced the familiar conundrum involving high-rise buildings and settling people on land well outside the city centre. Since they had enough money to buy a better parcel of land and build a basic structure, they put their funds into that. The land was bought and the houses were built with the main components

that families could not construct on their own: roof, kitchen and bathroom. Occupants were then left to complete the houses as and when they could.

Since that project, Elemental have completed others in a similar fashion, the most recent in Monterrey, Mexico. Using efficient prefabrication techniques along with clean, modern design, the firm create structures that are humane in purpose, appearance and scale. Modular, rectilinear forms cluster around a common open area that provides play space for children or community gatherings. The basic design consists of a three-storey building that contains a 'house' on the ground floor and a two-storey 'apartment' above. Both are built with void sections, which the residents can later complete on their own to expand their home.

In 2008 Aravena and his team won the Golden Lion award at the Milan Triennale for their prefabricated house prototype, which was inspired by the challenge to house one million people per week 'for the next twenty years, with a budget of only $10,000 per family'. This was based on the prediction that 'the number of people living in cities by 2030 will rise from three billion to five billion', an urbanization that 'will take place mainly in the poorest countries of the world'. With money available to build only half a house, the architect/builder constructs the more complex half (that requires services), while the residents do the rest. Void spaces can be filled in using the 'Tecno-panel' product developed for the Casa Elemental, a quick-build emergency shelter – another way in which, as Aravena puts it, architecture is used to both demonstrate creative skill and to solve the real and pressing problems of our communities.

The programme, as built in Monterrey, begins with a house on the ground floor and two-storey apartment above. Both can be expanded by filling in voids left to keep the initial construction budget viable. Basic kitchen and bathroom services are provided, while owners are encouraged to finish off the houses and expand living spaces as and when they are able.

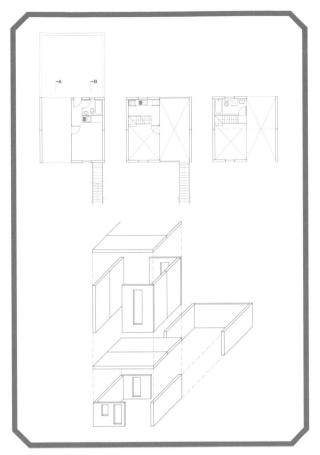

The Milan prototype house is based on an initial size of 18.6m² (194 sq ft), which can be expanded to 62.8m² (667 sq ft), and a duplex design that can expand from 26.3m² (280 sq ft) to 71.8m² (764 sq ft). The method combines the efficiency and economy of prefabrication with the individual customization provided by each family.

Overleaf: The government of Nuevo León in northwest Mexico commissioned seventy homes on a site of 0.6 hectares (1.5 acres) in the middle-class neighbourhood of Santa Catarina. Almost 50 per cent of the finished volume will be self-built.